IMAGE COMICS, INC. • **Robert Kirkman**: Chief Operating Officer • **Erik Larsen**: Chief Financial Officer • **Todd McFarlane**: President • **Marc Silvestri**: Chief Executive Officer • **Jim Valentino**: Vice President • **Eric Stephenson**: Publisher / Chief Creative Officer • **Corey Hart**: Director of Sales • **Jeff Boison**: Director of Publishing Planning & Book Trade Sales • **Chris Ross**: Director of Digital Sales • **Jeff Stang**: Director of Specialty Sales • **Kat Salazar**: Director of PR & Marketing • **Drew Gill**: Art Director • **Heather Doornink**: Production Director • **Nicole Lapalme**: Controller • **IMAGECOMICS.COM**

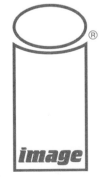

EAST OF WEST

JONATHAN HICKMAN
WRITER

NICK DRAGOTTA
ARTIST

FRANK MARTIN
COLORS

RUS WOOTON
LETTERS

EAS

W

T OF

EST

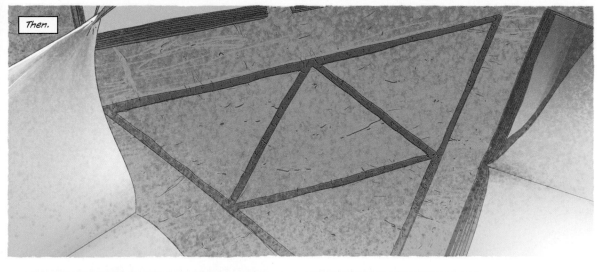

Then.

This... this is...

Unexpected, I know.

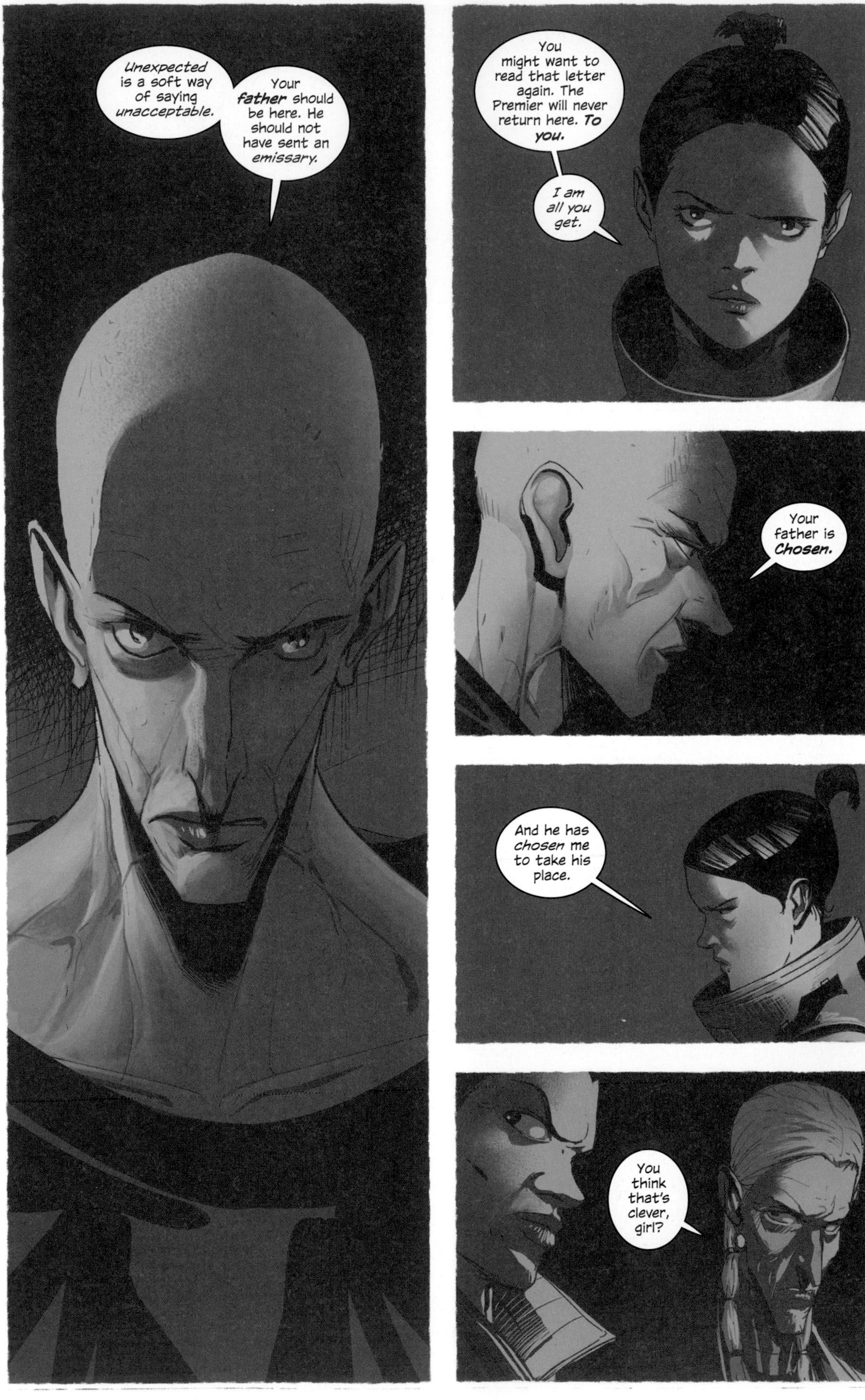

Unexpected is a soft way of saying *unacceptable.*
Your **father** should be here. He should not have sent an *emissary.*
You might want to read that letter again. The Premier will never return here. ***To you.***
I am all you get.
Your father is **Chosen.**
And he has *chosen* me to take his place.
You think that's clever, girl?

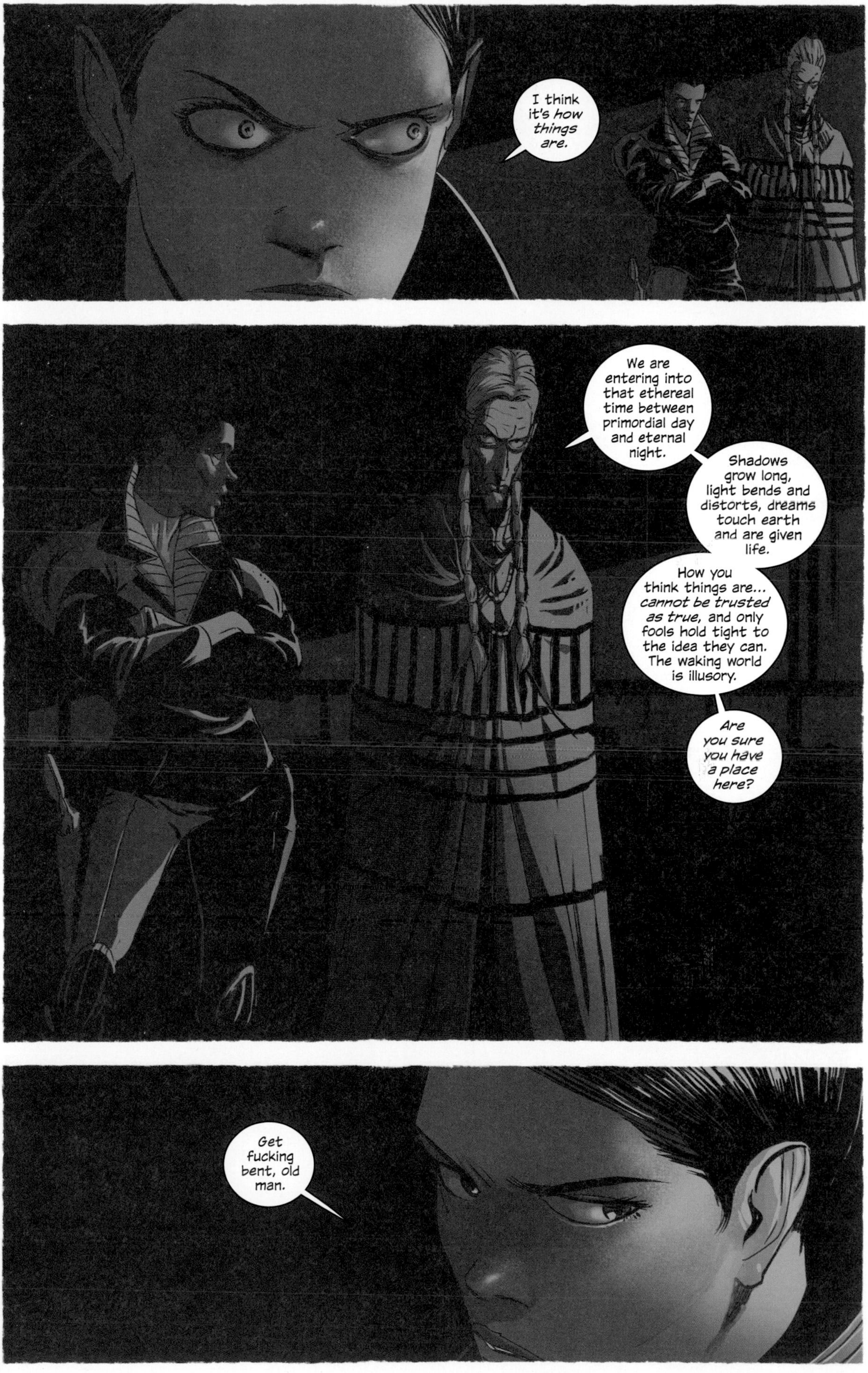
I think it's *how things are.*
We are entering into that ethereal time between primordial day and eternal night.
Shadows grow long, light bends and distorts, dreams touch earth and are given life.
How you think things are... *cannot be trusted as true*, and only fools hold tight to the idea they can. The waking world is illusory.
Are you sure you have a place here?
Get fucking bent, old man.

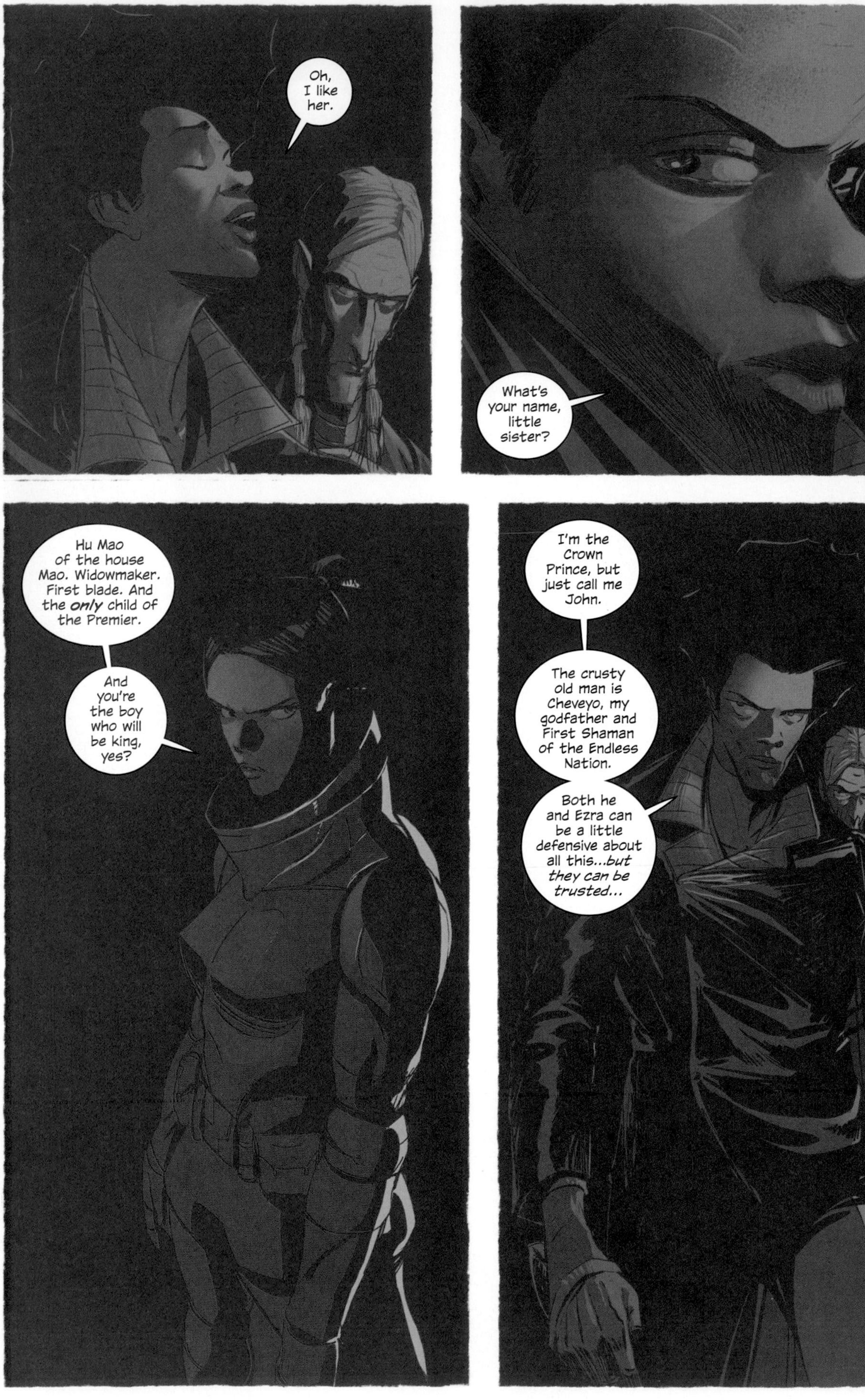

Oh, I like her.
What's your name, little sister?
Hu Mao of the house Mao. Widowmaker. First blade. And the *only* child of the Premier.
And you're the boy who will be king, yes?
I'm the Crown Prince, but just call me John.
The crusty old man is Cheveyo, my godfather and First Shaman of the Endless Nation.
Both he and Ezra can be a little defensive about all this...*but they can be trusted...*

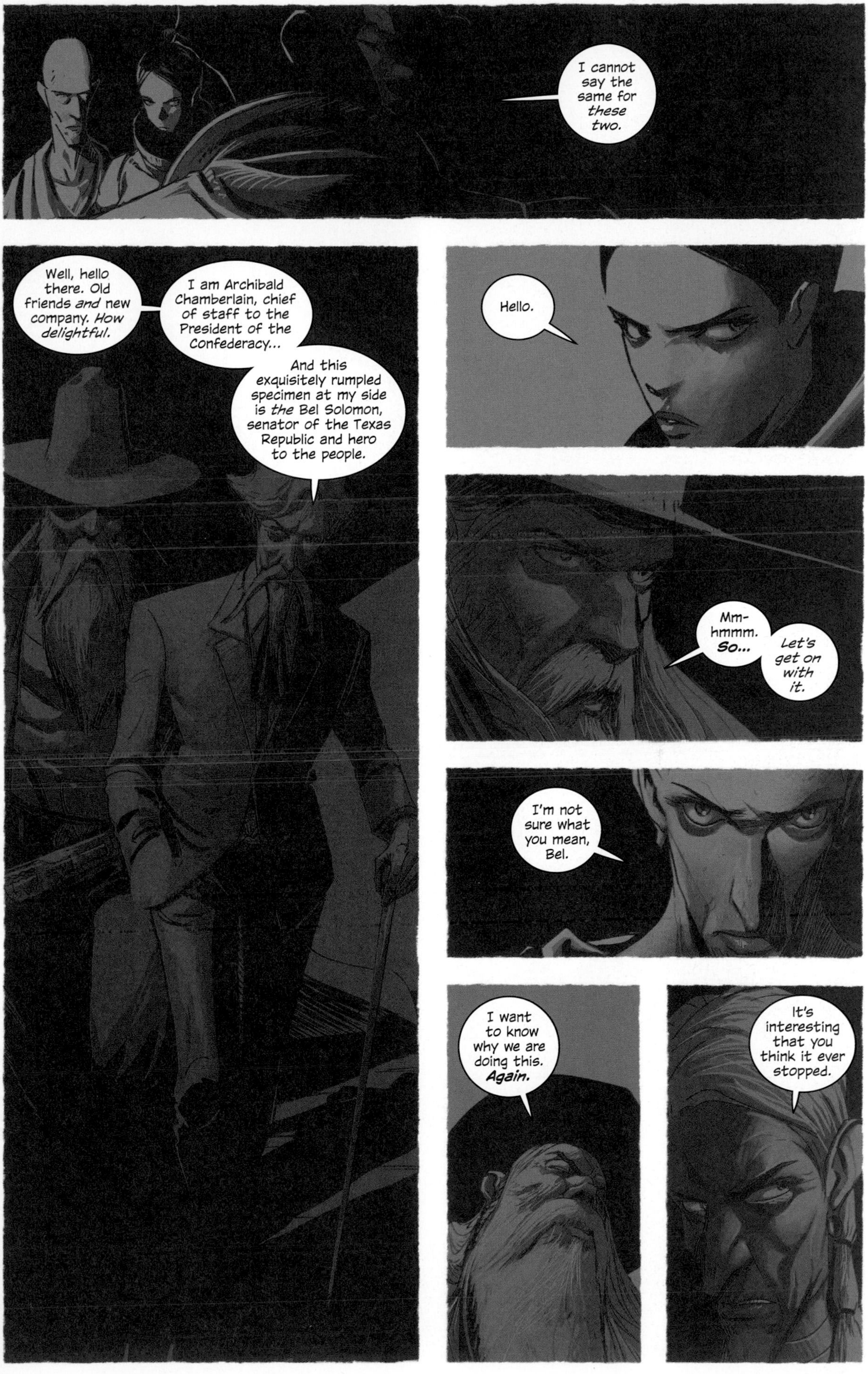
I cannot say the same for *these two.*
Well, hello there. Old friends *and* new company. *How delightful.*
I am Archibald Chamberlain, chief of staff to the President of the Confederacy...
And this exquisitely rumpled specimen at my side is *the* Bel Solomon, senator of the Texas Republic and hero to the people.
Hello.
Mm-hmmm. **So...**
Let's get on with it.
I'm not sure what you mean, Bel.
I want to know why we are doing this. ***Again.***
It's interesting that you think it ever stopped.

You mean the *good work* of bringing about the *rightful end* of the world?

Be it fire. Be it flood. We Chosen serve the Message and that message is the end of all things.

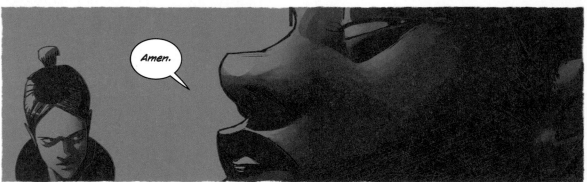

Amen.

So. First day on the job?

It is.

Everything you expected?

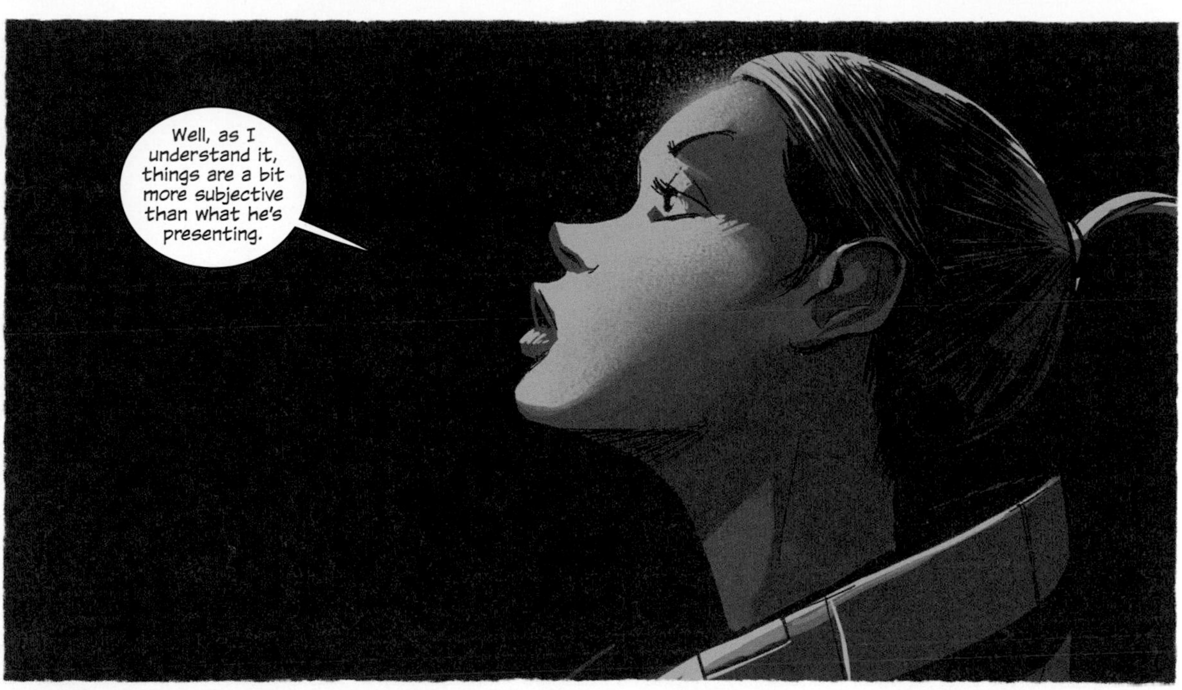
Well, as I understand it, things are a bit more subjective than what he's presenting.

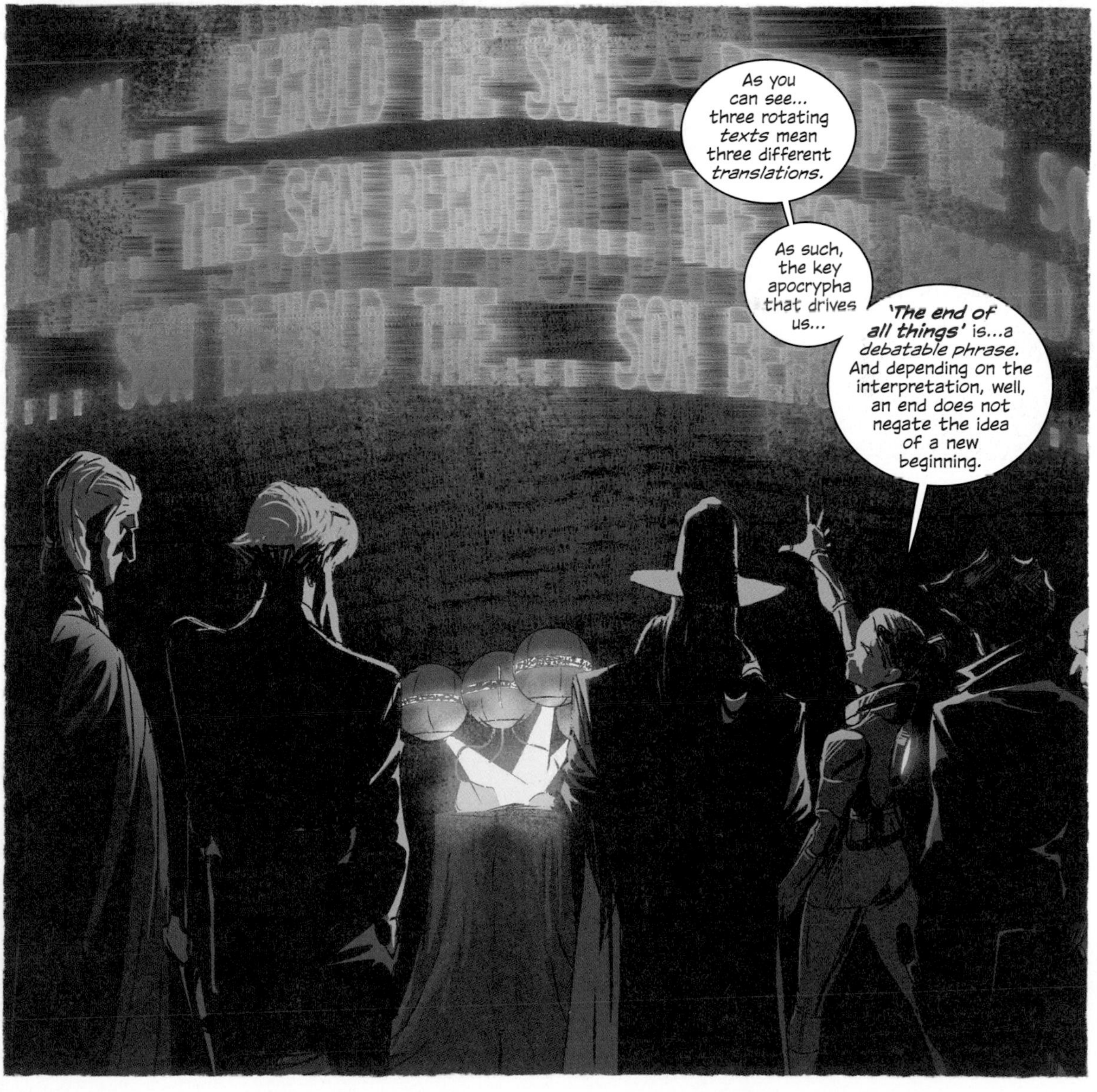
BEHOLD THE SON...
THE SON BEHOLD...
SON BEHOLD THE...
As you can see... three rotating *texts* mean three different *translations.*
As such, the key apocrypha that drives us...
'The end of all things' is...a *debatable phrase.* And depending on the interpretation, well, an end does not negate the idea of a new beginning.

Dear god, woman. Are you daring to introduce some small sliver of hope into this place?

I am here to serve. *That's all.*

Are you buying this?

Hrmpt!

And you?

Cheveyo would not agree with what she says...

That is truth. *I would not.*

But I would. So there's your answer, Bel. Do with it what you will.

Well, I admit, that's all good and goddamn fascinating...

But you're all forgetting one thing: *The Message* is just a guide -- but what we actually served was a *higher power.*

The reason we haven't met, talked, or acted on it for ten years is because that higher power is dead, and it happened right in front of us.

We all watched.

So I don't want to hear about the end times, and I don't want to hear about the word...

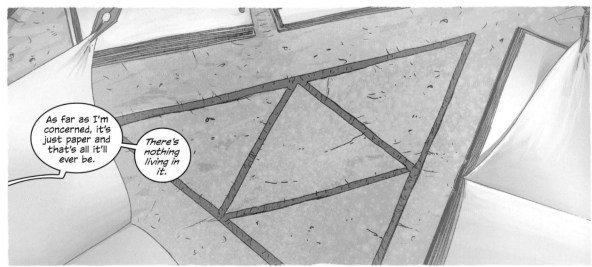

As far as I'm concerned, it's just paper and that's all it'll ever be.

There's nothing living in it.

HOW THINGS **WERE** IS
NOT HOW THEY WILL
ALWAYS **BE** .

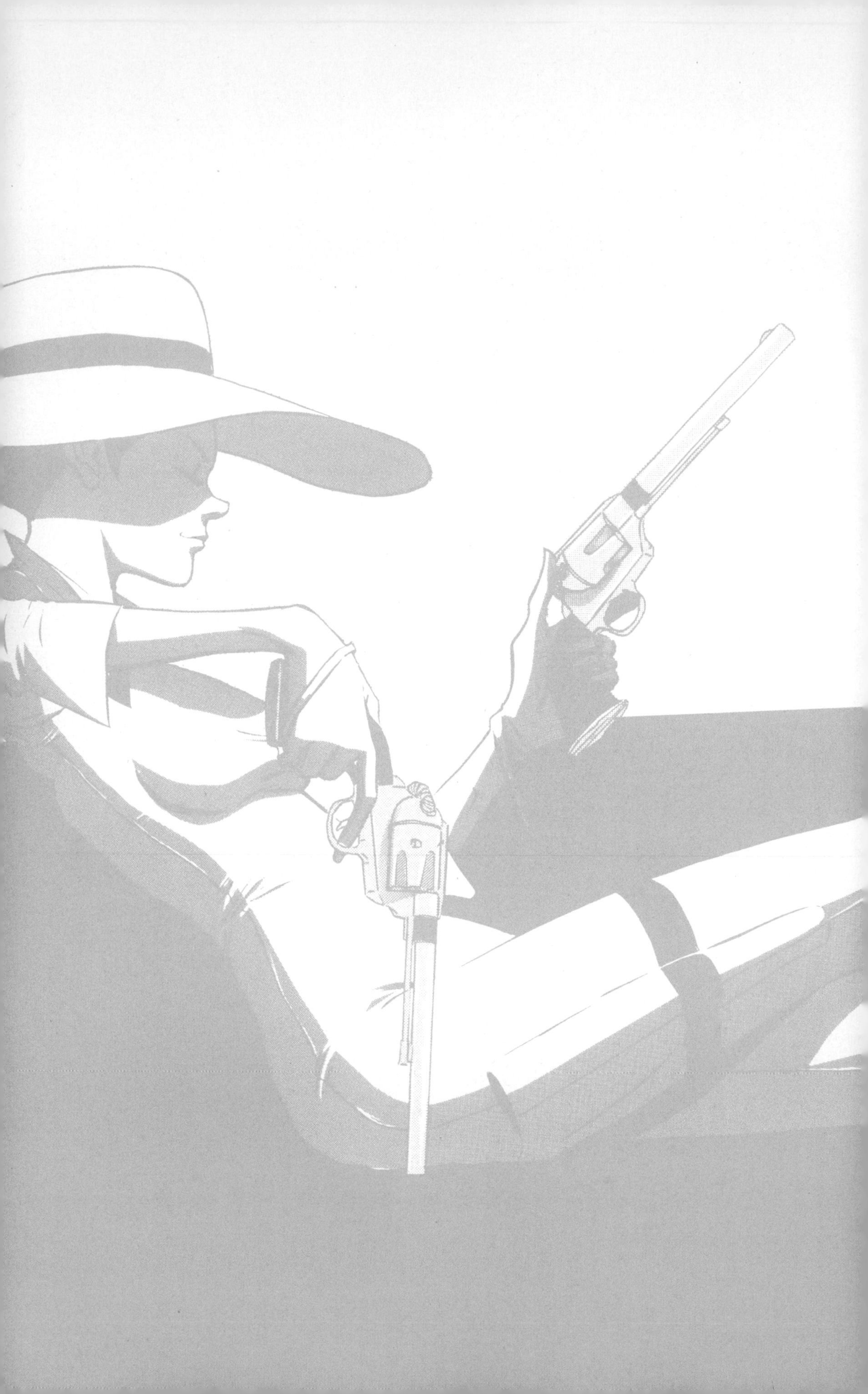

39

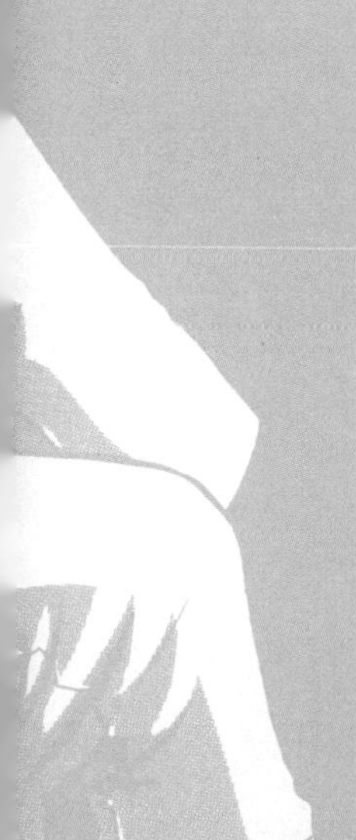

THIRTY-NINE:
THE **THREE** ARE
ONE

HOW THINGS **ARE** IS NOT
HOW THEY WILL **END**.

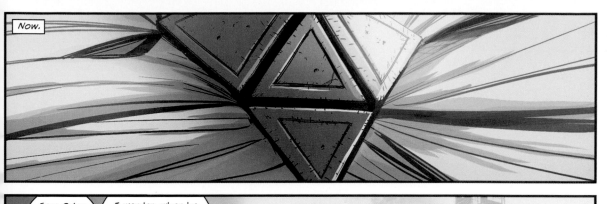

Now.

Ezra Orion ate the Message and became the word.

I wonder, when he closed his eyes, did he see his end between my teeth, or was he blind to his fate -- a pawn of forces beyond his control.

I wonder, am I?

Hrmpt!

What's got you in a mood, love?

I feel the word moving in me, Crow.

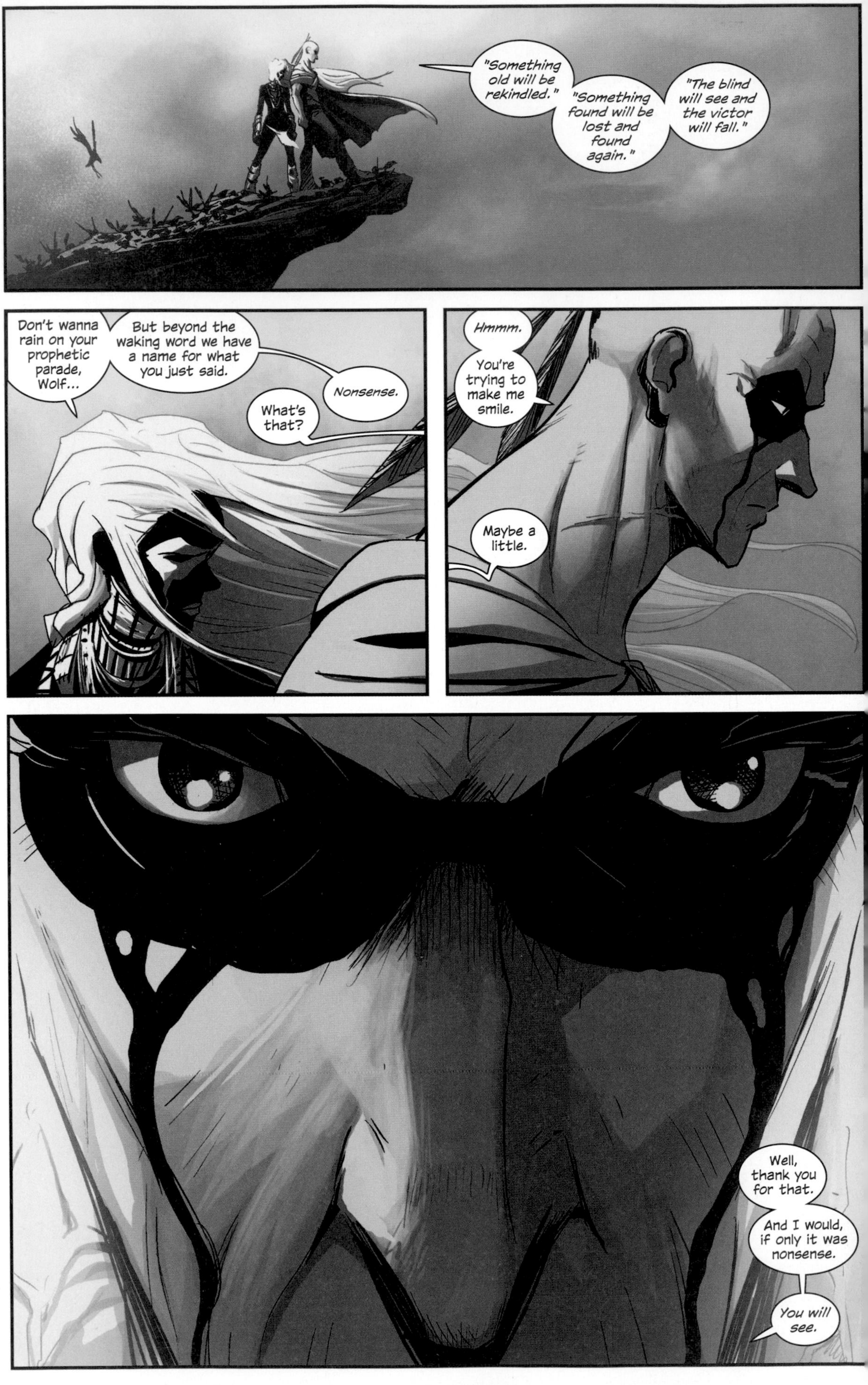
"Something old will be rekindled."
"Something found will be lost and found again."
"The blind will see and the victor will fall."
Don't wanna rain on your prophetic parade, Wolf...
But beyond the waking word we have a name for what you just said.
Nonsense.
What's that?
Hmmm.
You're trying to make me smile.
Maybe a little.
Well, thank you for that.
And I would, if only it was nonsense.
You will see.

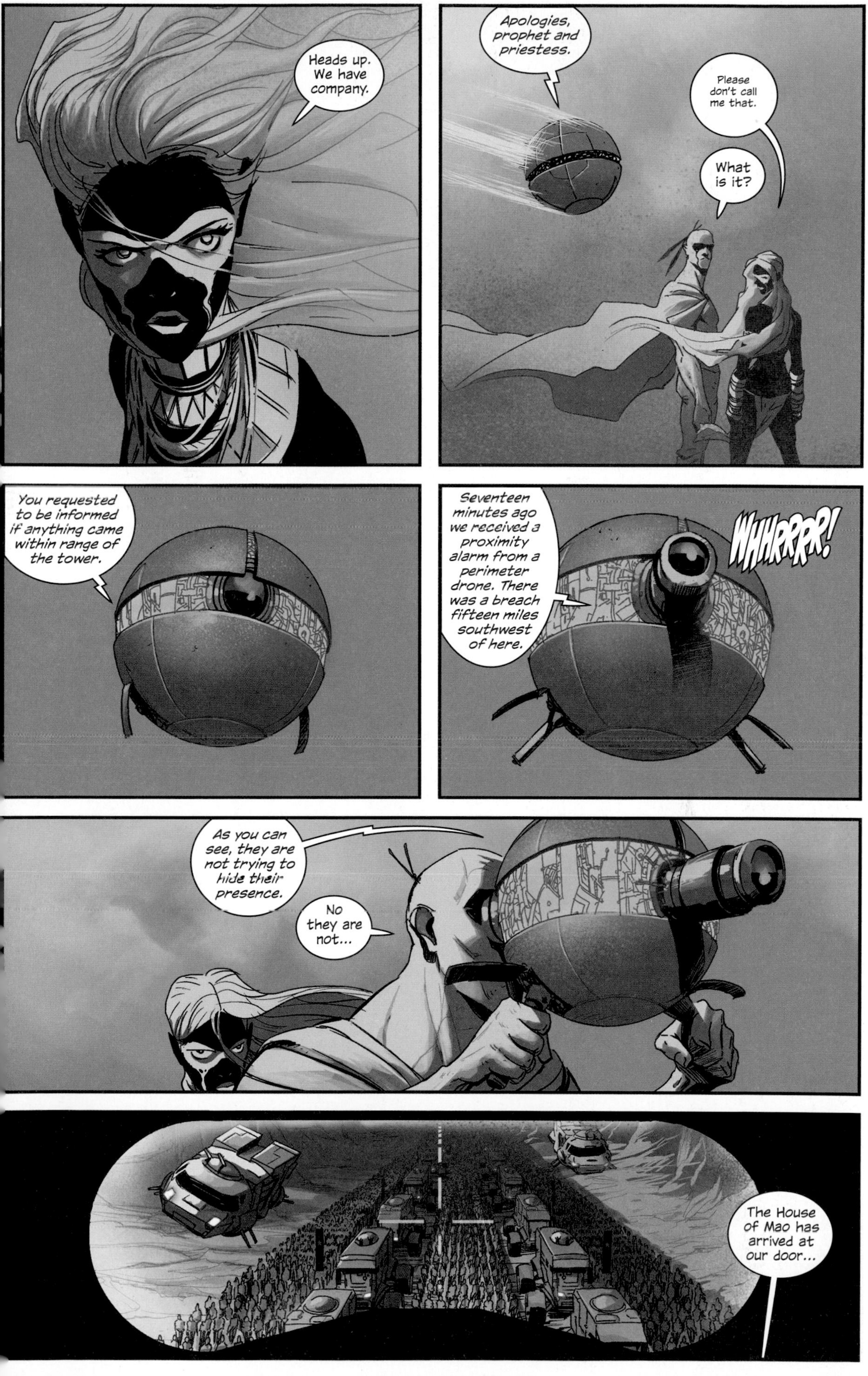
Heads up. We have company.
Apologies, prophet and priestess.
Please don't call me that.
What is it?
You requested to be informed if anything came within range of the tower.
Seventeen minutes ago we received a proximity alarm from a perimeter drone. There was a breach fifteen miles southwest of here.
WHHRRRR!
As you can see, they are not trying to hide their presence.
No they are not...
The House of Mao has arrived at our door...

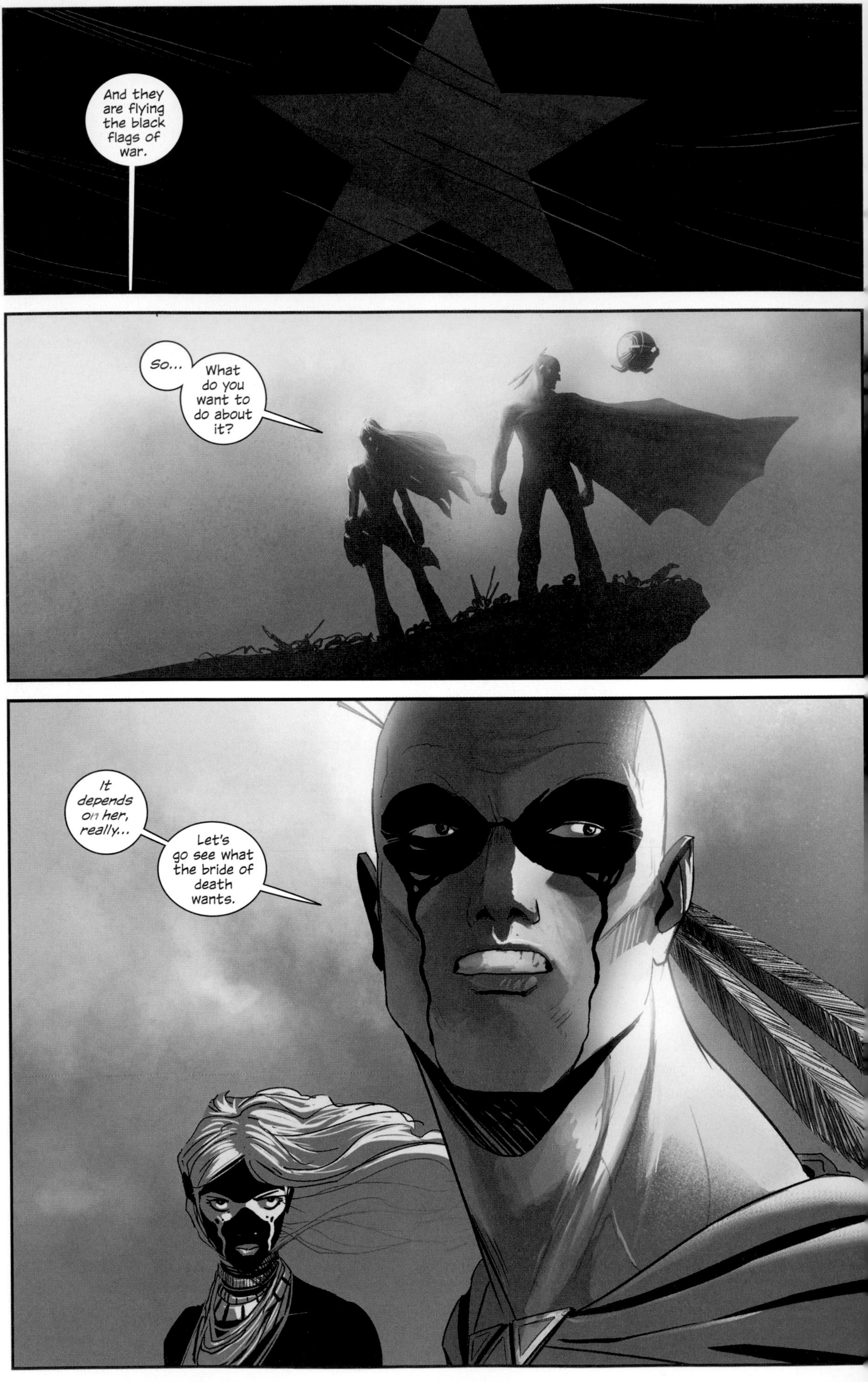
And they are flying the black flags of war.
So...
What do you want to do about it?
It depends on her, really...
Let's go see what the bride of death wants.

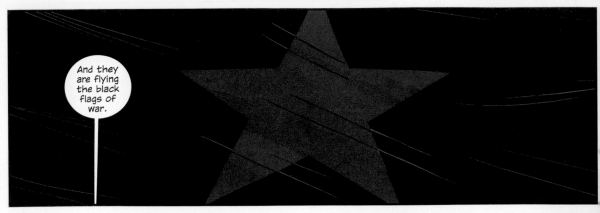

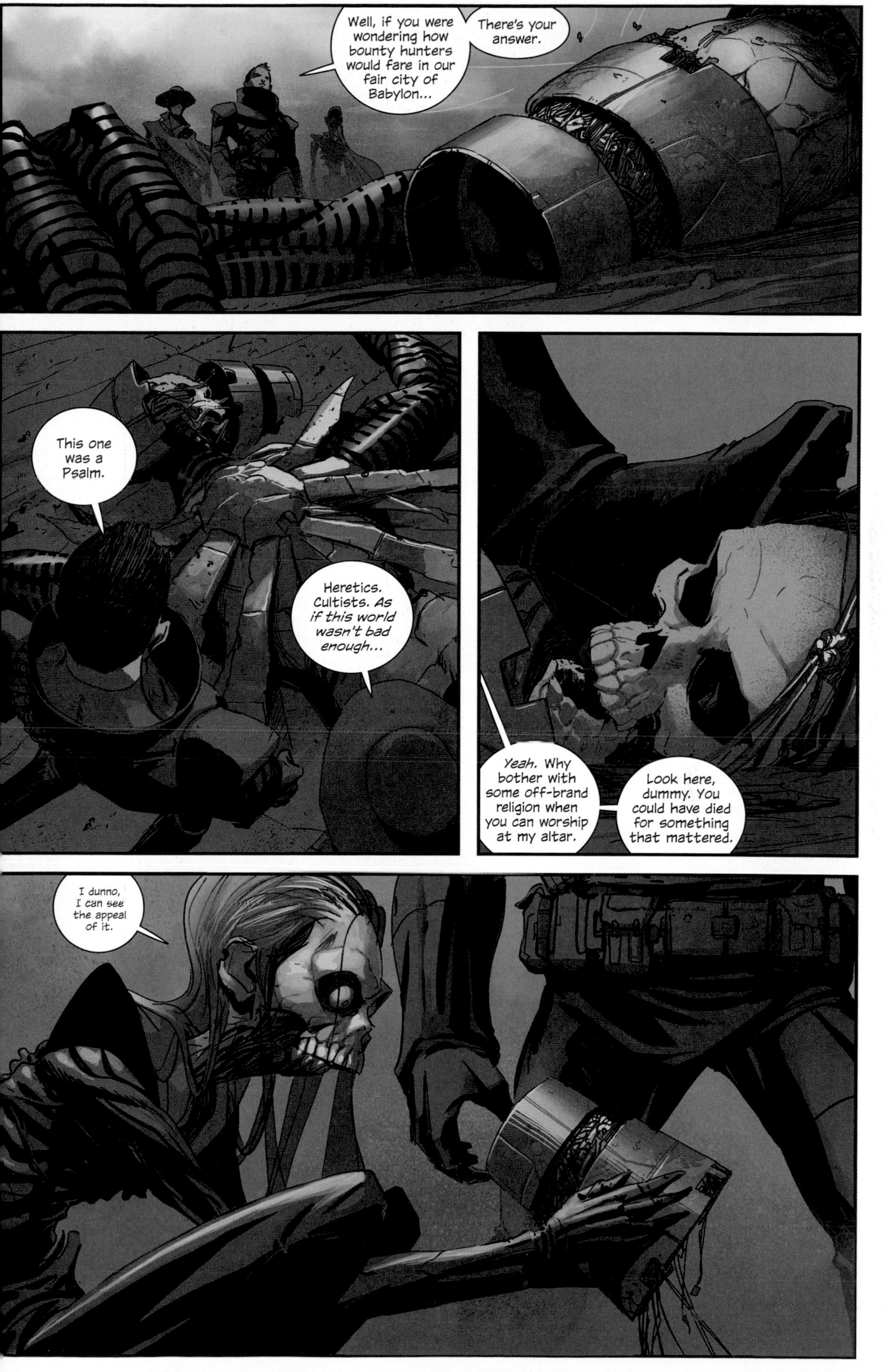
Well, if you were wondering how bounty hunters would fare in our fair city of Babylon...
There's your answer.
This one was a Psalm.
Heretics. Cultists. *As if this world wasn't bad enough...*
Yeah. Why bother with some off-brand religion when you can worship at my altar.
Look here, dummy. You could have died for something that mattered.
I dunno, I can see the appeal of it.

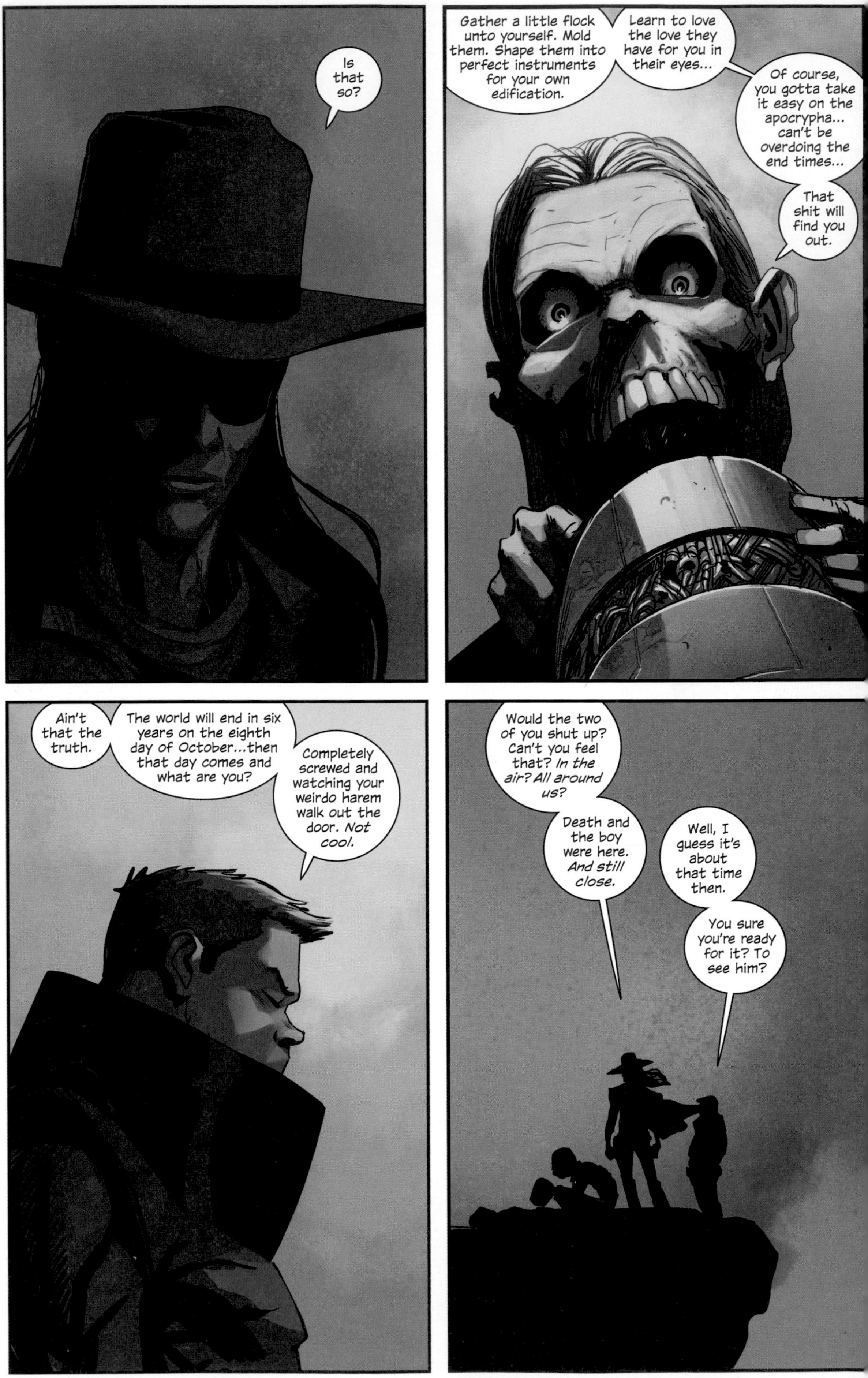
Is that so?
Gather a little flock unto yourself. Mold them. Shape them into perfect instruments for your own edification.
Learn to love the love they have for you in their eyes...
Of course, you gotta take it easy on the apocrypha... can't be overdoing the end times...
That shit will find you out.
Ain't that the truth.
The world will end in six years on the eighth day of October...then that day comes and what are you?
Completely screwed and watching your weirdo harem walk out the door. *Not cool.*
Would the two of you shut up? Can't you feel that? *In the air? All around us?*
Death and the boy were here. *And still close.*
Well, I guess it's about that time then.
You sure you're ready for it? To see him?

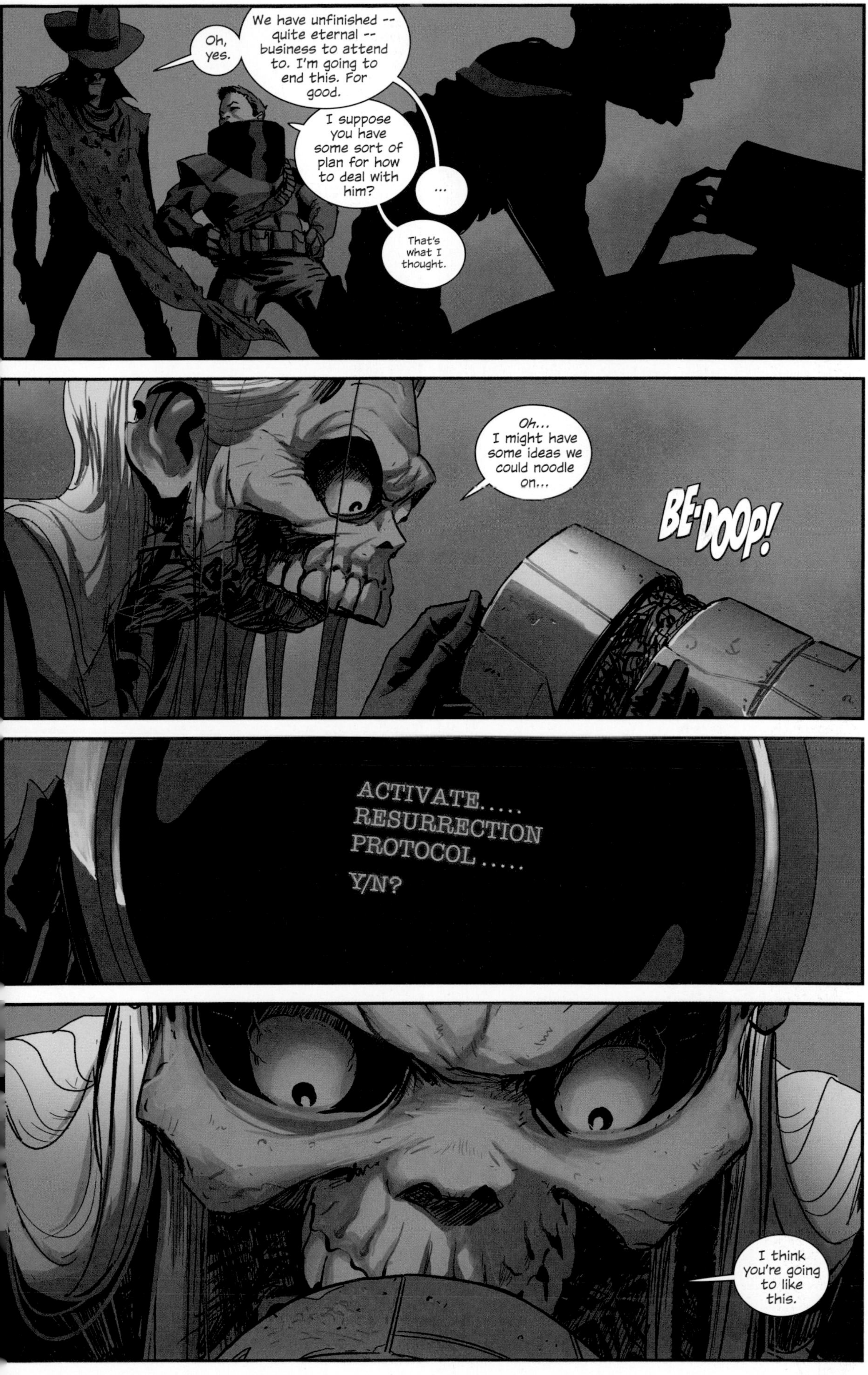
Oh, yes.
We have unfinished -- quite eternal -- business to attend to. I'm going to end this. For good.
I suppose you have some sort of plan for how to deal with him?
...
That's what I thought.
Oh... I might have some ideas we could noodle on...
BE-DOOP!
ACTIVATE..... RESURRECTION PROTOCOL..... Y/N?
I think you're going to like this.

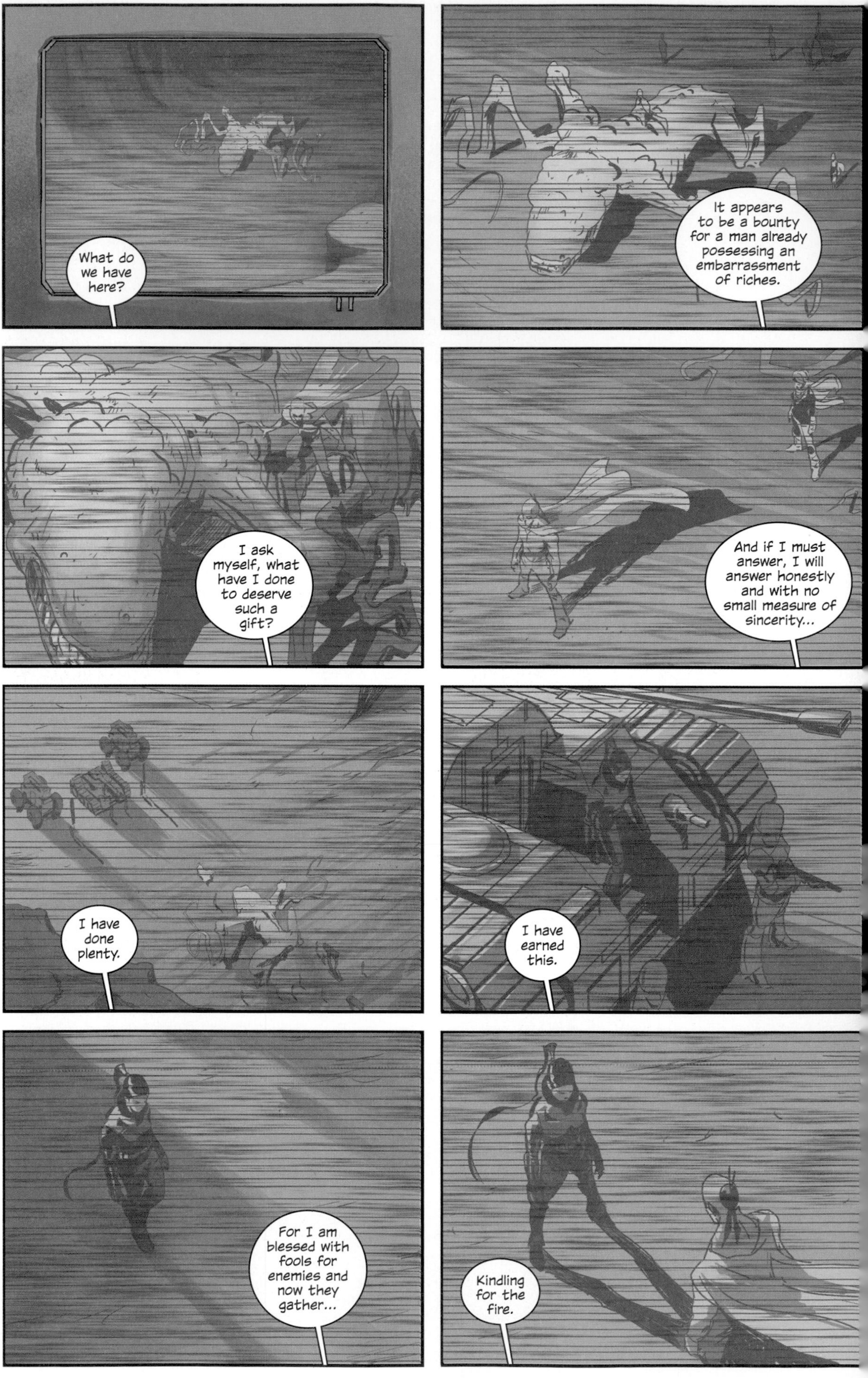
What do we have here?
It appears to be a bounty for a man already possessing an embarrassment of riches.
I ask myself, what have I done to deserve such a gift?
And if I must answer, I will answer honestly and with no small measure of sincerity...
I have done plenty.
I have earned this.
For I am blessed with fools for enemies and now they gather...
Kindling for the fire.

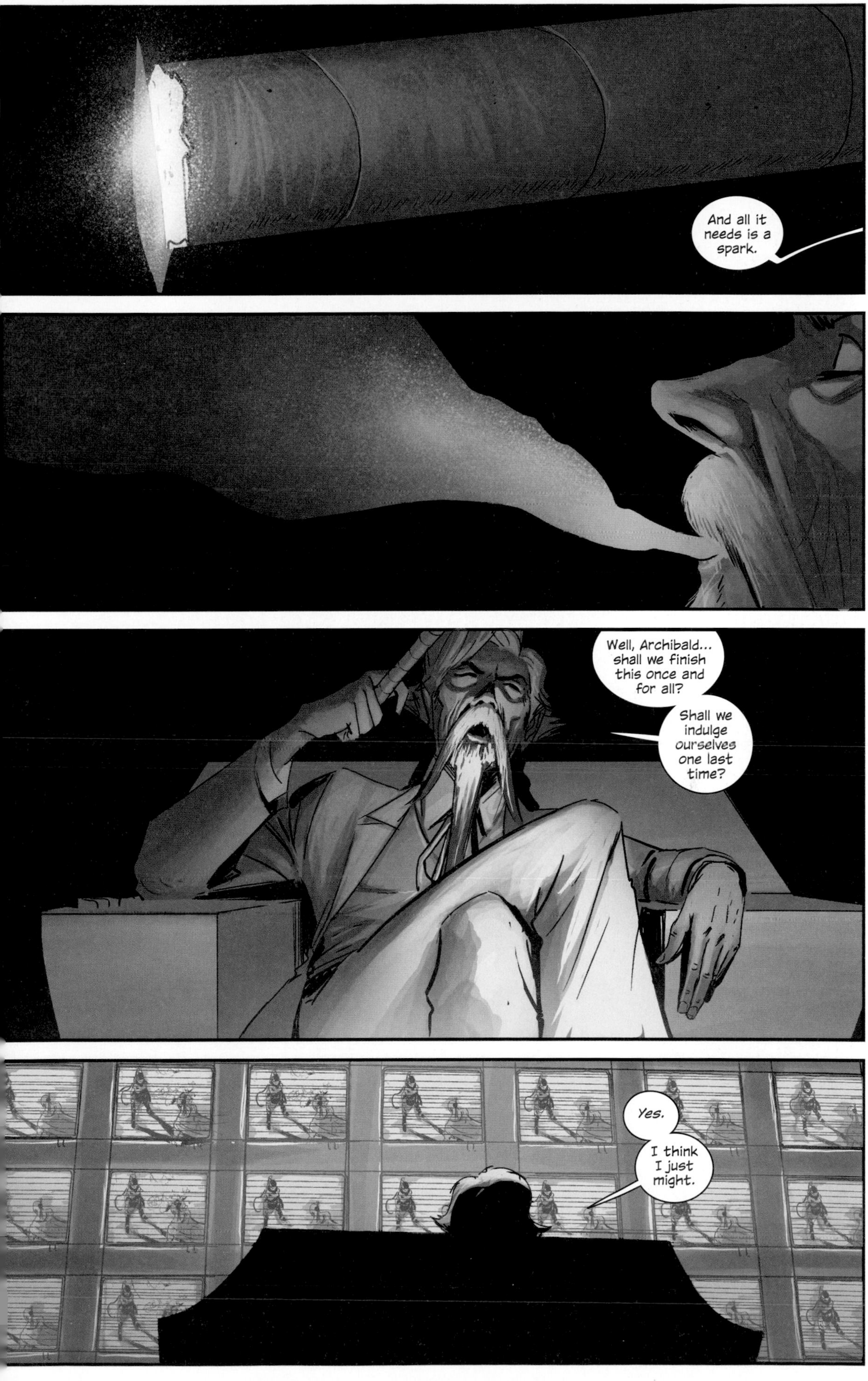
And all it needs is a spark.
Well, Archibald... shall we finish this once and for all?
Shall we indulge ourselves one last time?
Yes.
I think I just might.

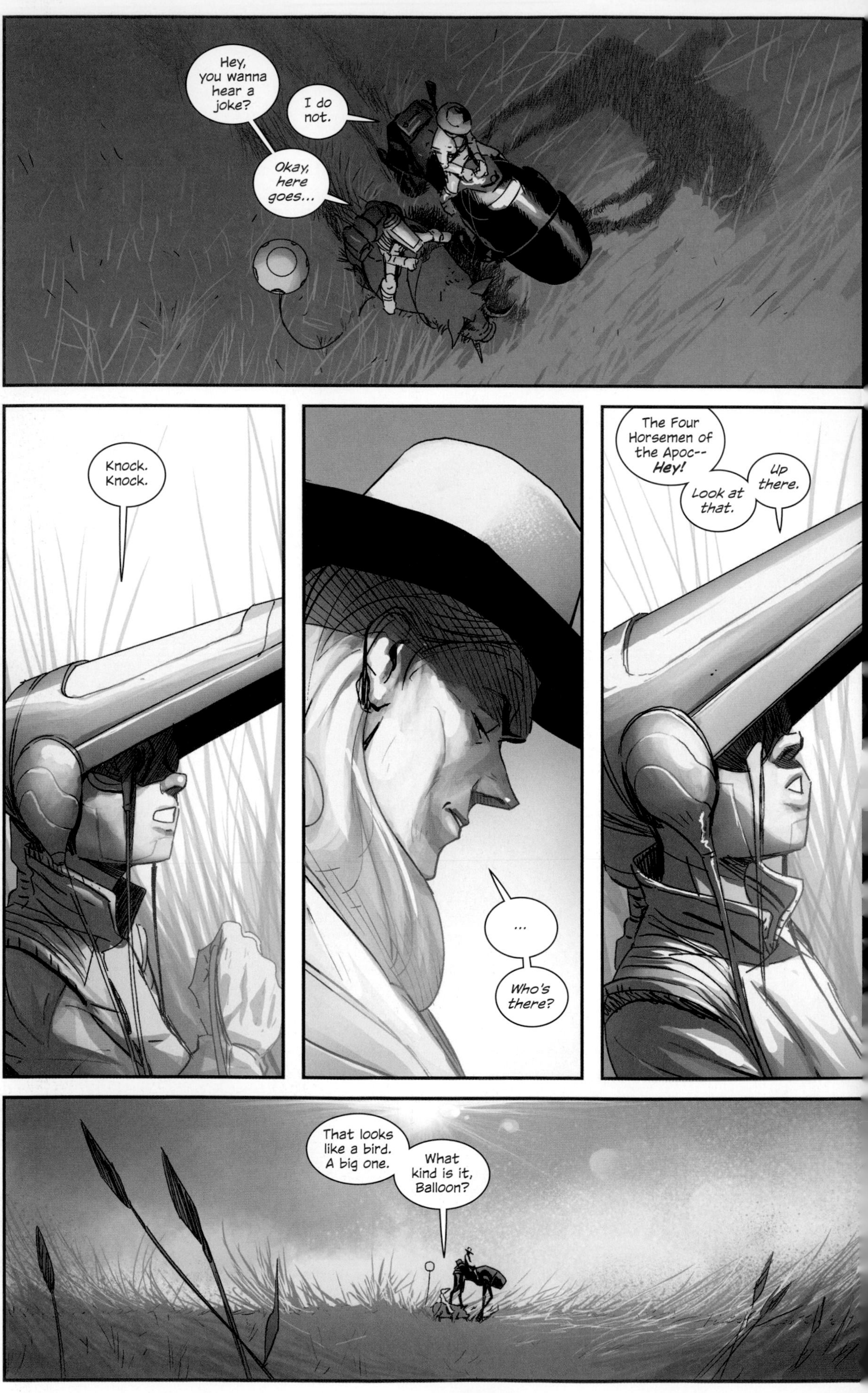
Hey, you wanna hear a joke?
I do not.
Okay, here goes...
Knock. Knock.
...
Who's there?
The Four Horsemen of the Apoc-- *Hey!*
Look at that.
Up there.
That looks like a bird. A big one.
What kind is it, Balloon?

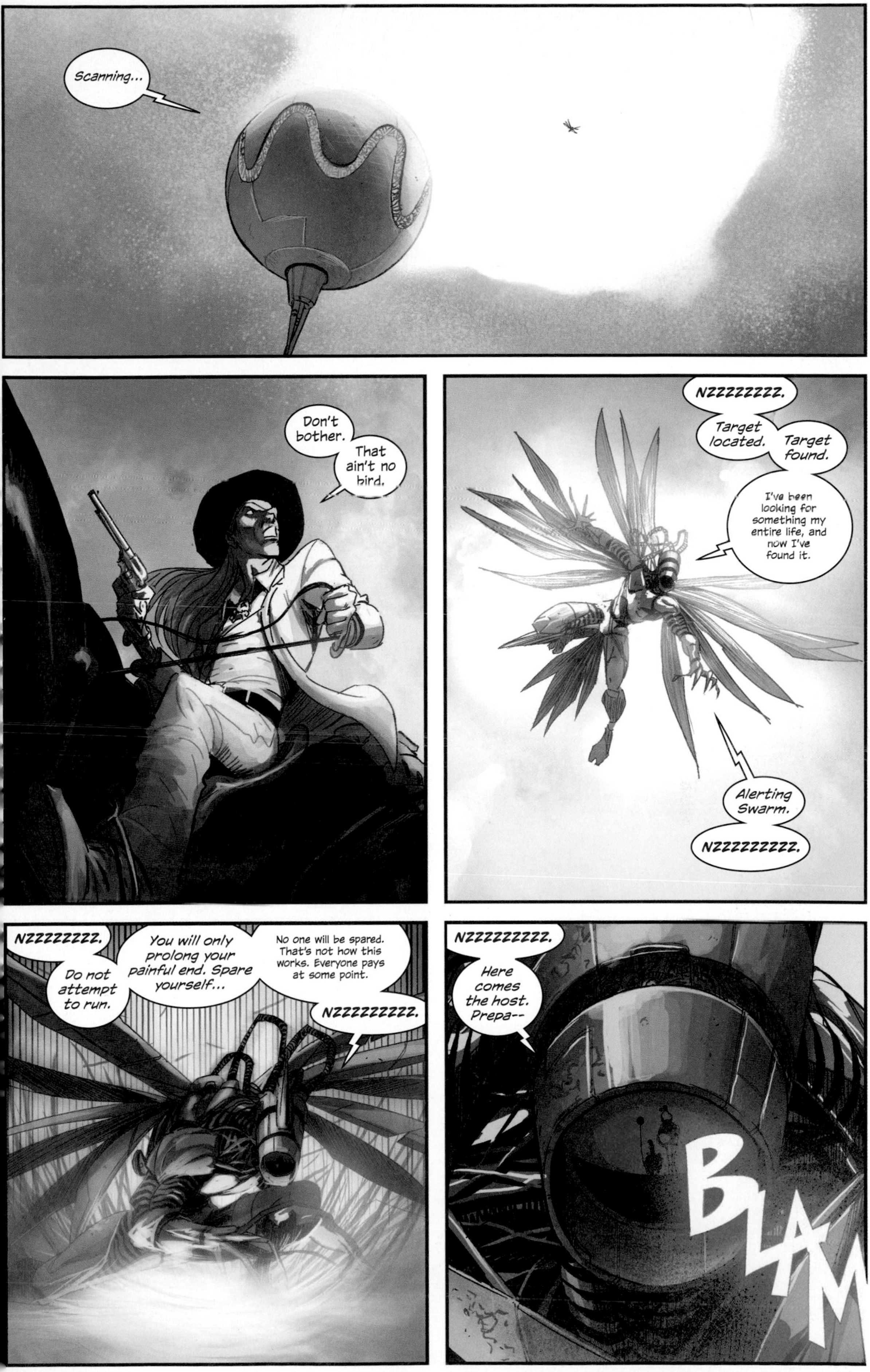
Scanning...
Don't bother. That ain't no bird.
NZZZZZZZZ.
Target located.
Target found.
I've been looking for something my entire life, and now I've found it.
Alerting Swarm.
NZZZZZZZZZ.
NZZZZZZZZ.
Do not attempt to run.
You will only prolong your painful end. Spare yourself...
No one will be spared. That's not how this works. Everyone pays at some point.
NZZZZZZZZZ.
NZZZZZZZZZ.
Here comes the host. Prepa--
BLAM

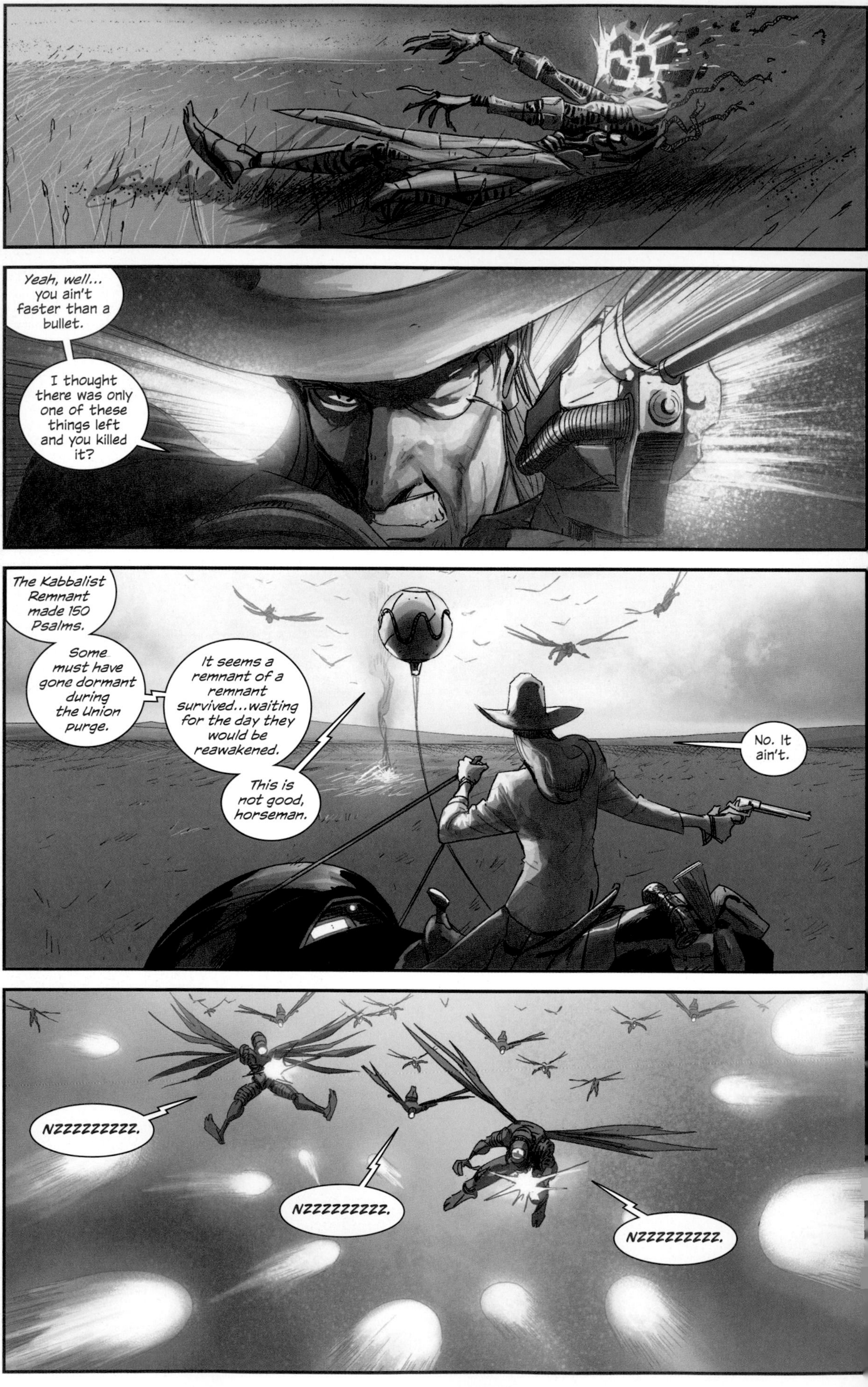
Yeah, well... you ain't faster than a bullet.
I thought there was only one of these things left and you killed it?
The Kabbalist Remnant made 150 Psalms.
Some must have gone dormant during the Union purge.
It seems a remnant of a remnant survived...waiting for the day they would be reawakened.
This is not good, horseman.
No. It ain't.
NZZZZZZZZZ.
NZZZZZZZZZ.
NZZZZZZZZZ.

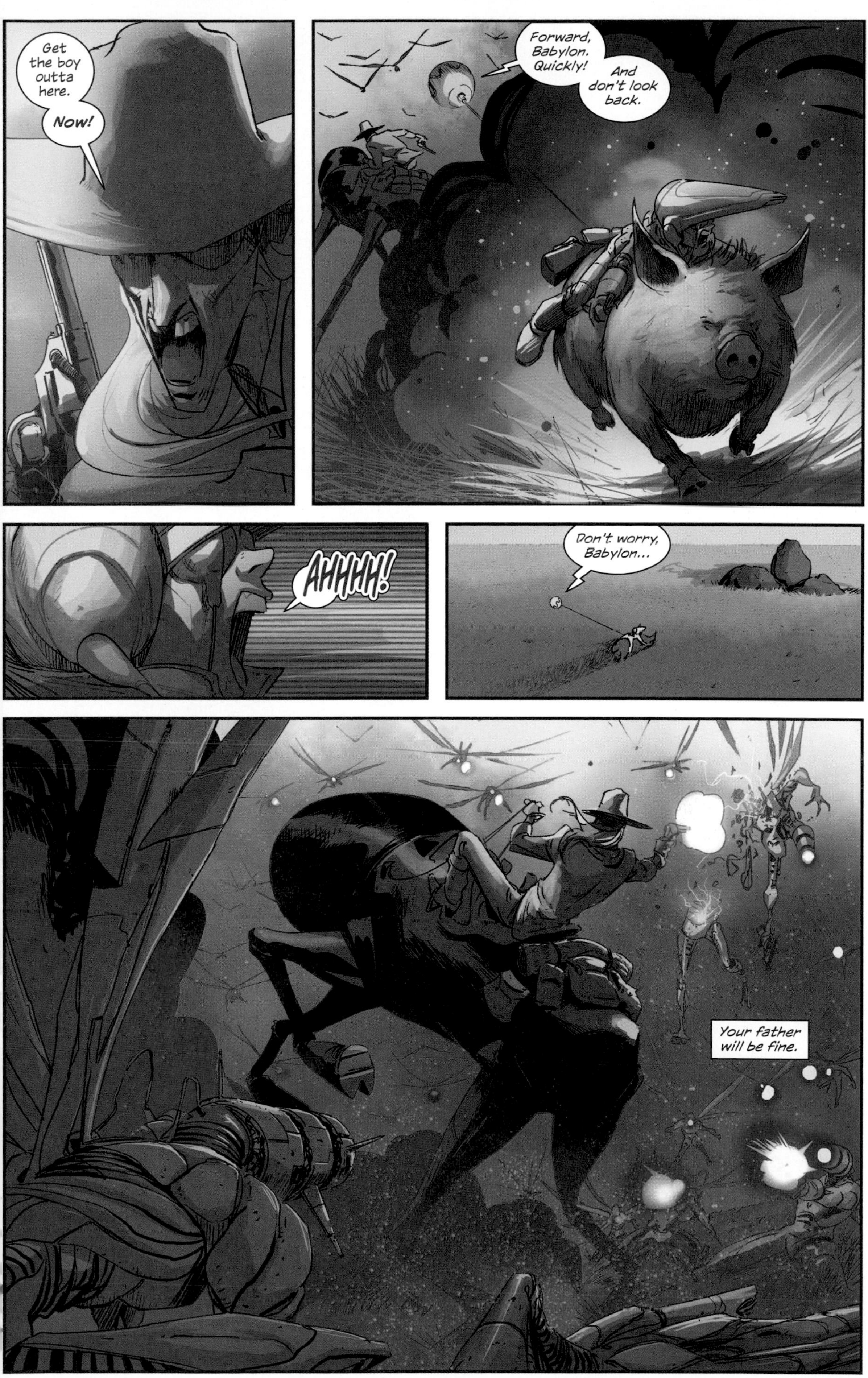

Get the boy outta here.
Now!
Forward, Babylon. Quickly!
And don't look back.
AHHHH!
Don't worry, Babylon...
Your father will be fine.

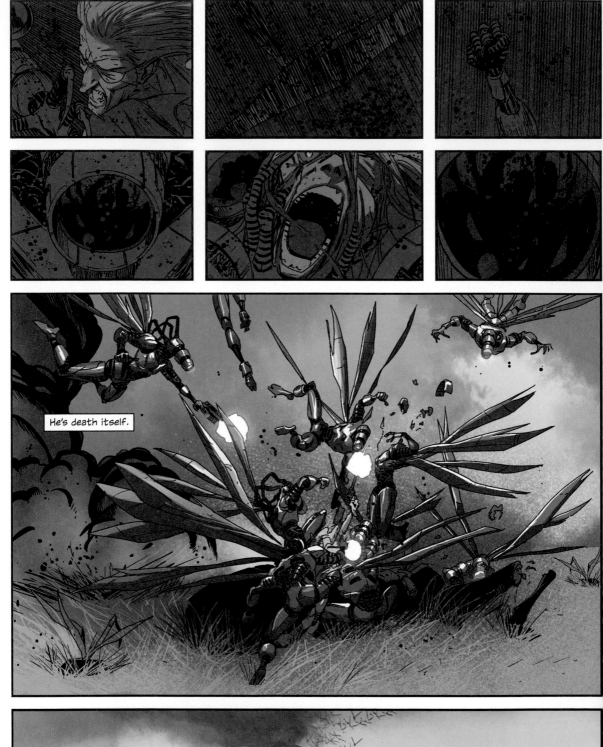

He's death itself.

What can stand against that?

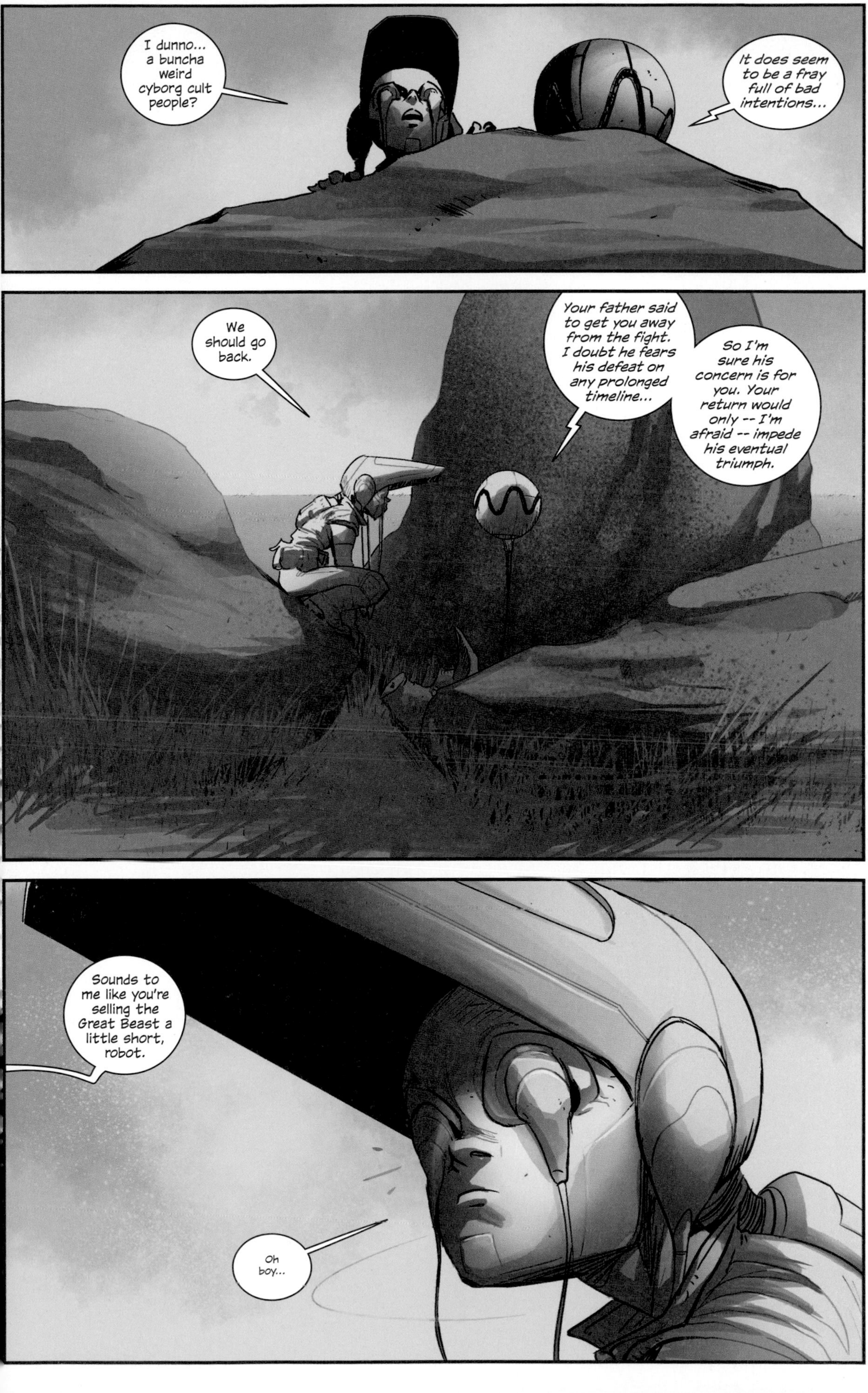
I dunno... a buncha weird cyborg cult people?
It does seem to be a fray full of bad intentions...
We should go back.
Your father said to get you away from the fight. I doubt he fears his defeat on any prolonged timeline...
So I'm sure his concern is for you. Your return would only -- I'm afraid -- impede his eventual triumph.
Sounds to me like you're selling the Great Beast a little short, robot.
Oh boy...

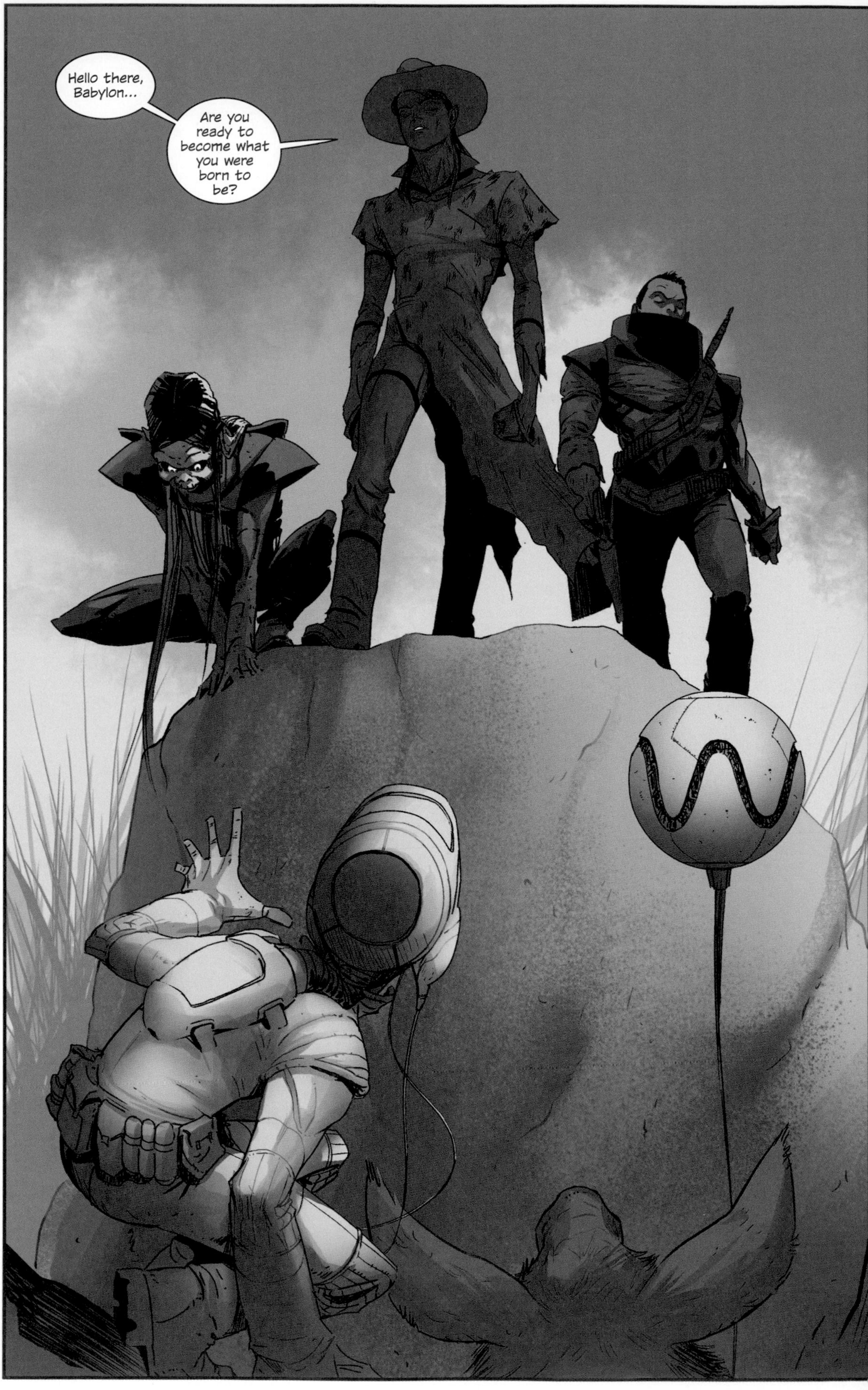
Hello there, Babylon...
Are you ready to become what you were born to be?

THE **NOW**
ALWAYS DISTORTS THE MEMORY
OF **HOW THINGS REALLY WERE.**

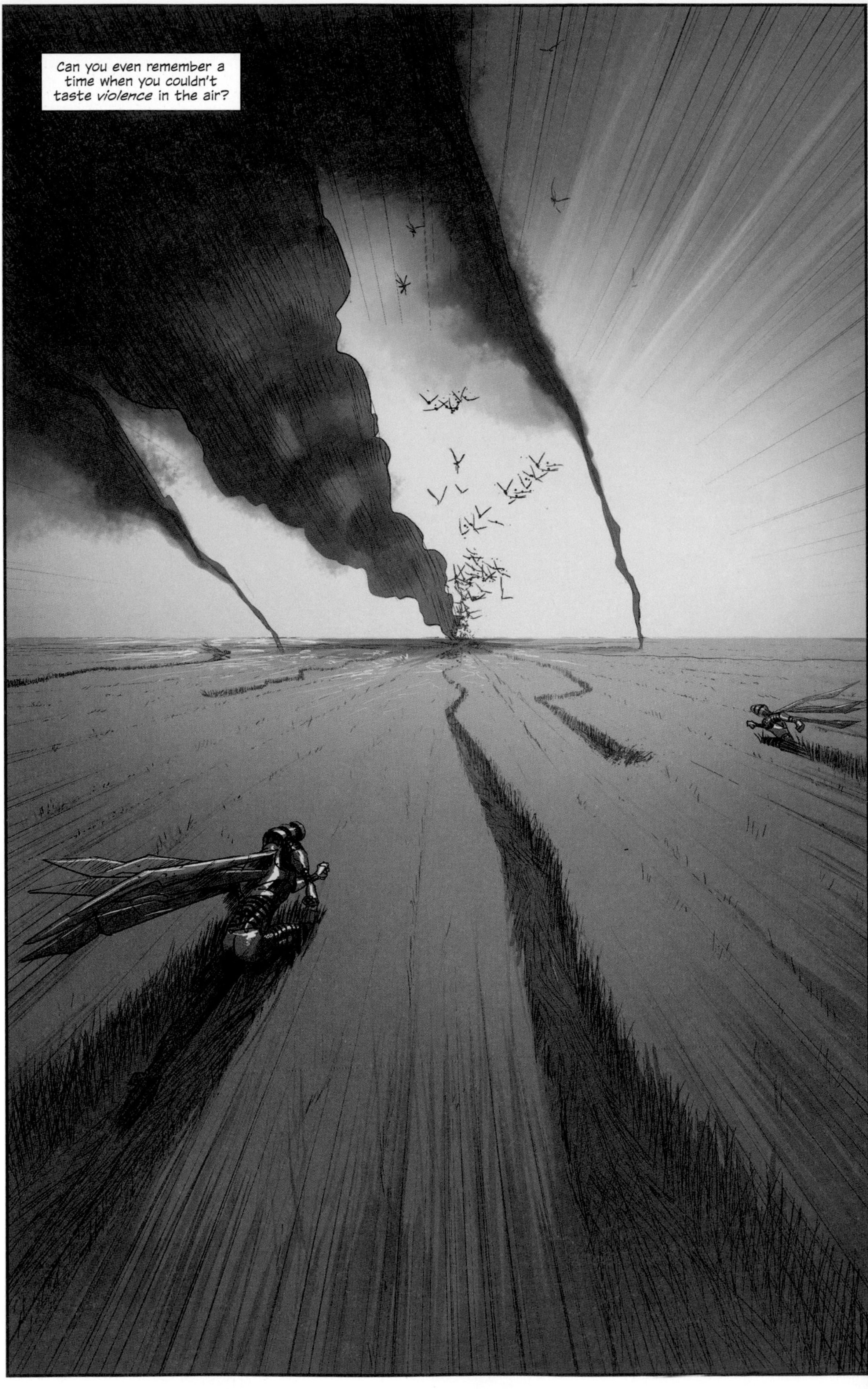
Can you even remember a time when you couldn't taste *violence* in the air?

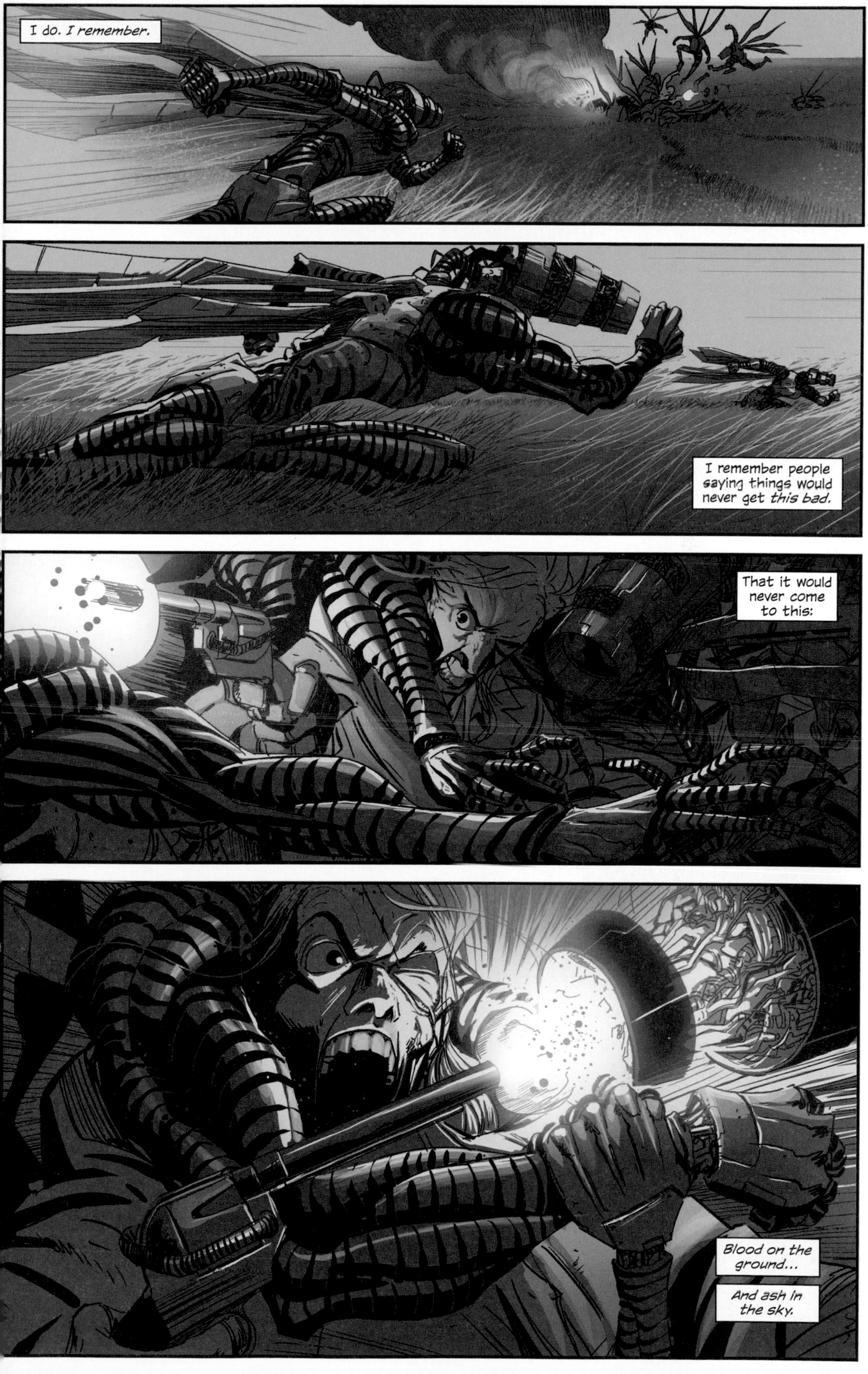
I do. *I remember.*
I remember people saying things would never get *this bad.*
That it would never come to this:
Blood on the ground...
And ash in the sky.

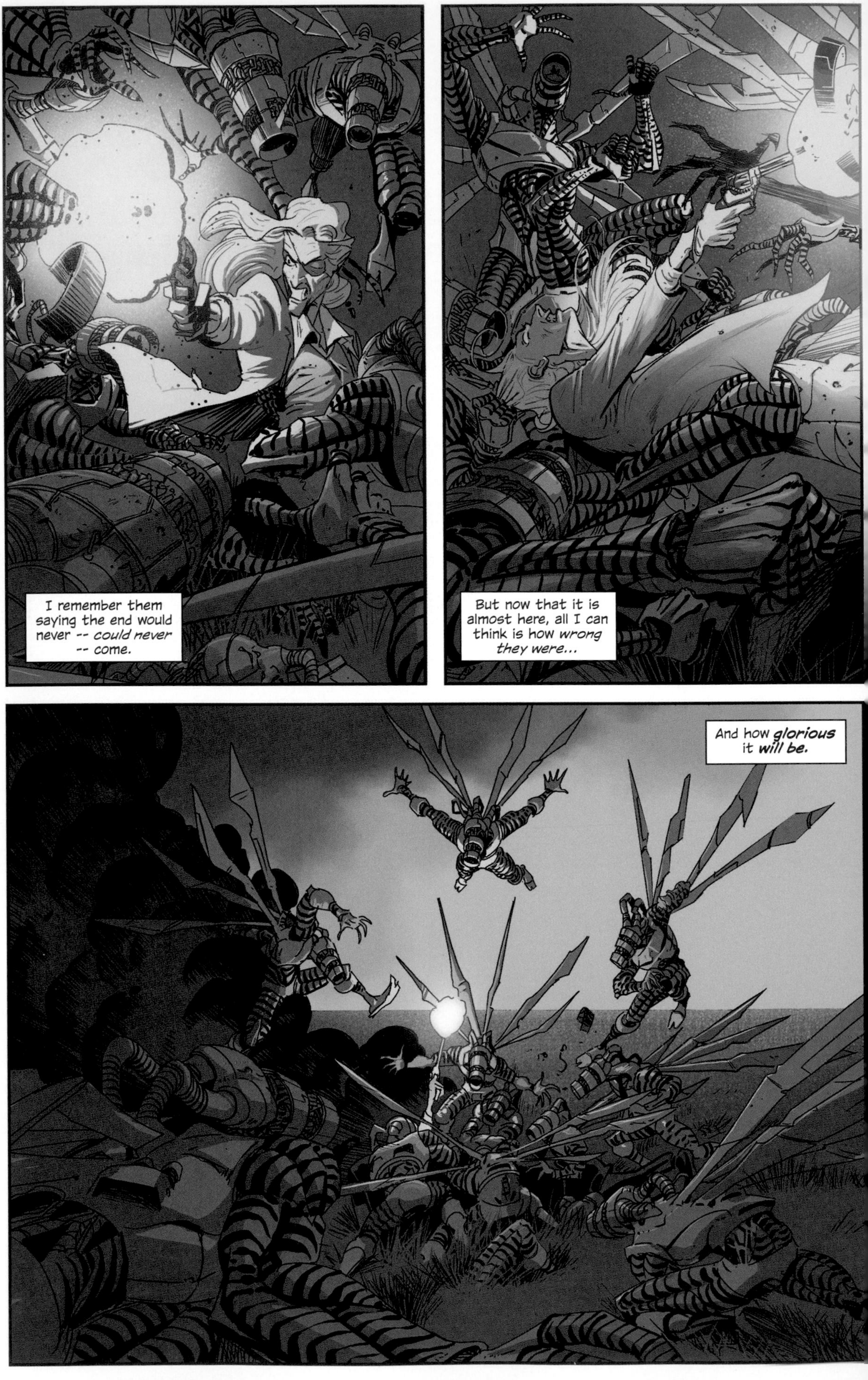
I remember them saying the end would never -- *could never* -- come.
But now that it is almost here, all I can think is how *wrong* they were...
And how ***glorious*** it ***will be.***

WE WILL SEE THIS THROUGH
TO THE **BITTER END.**

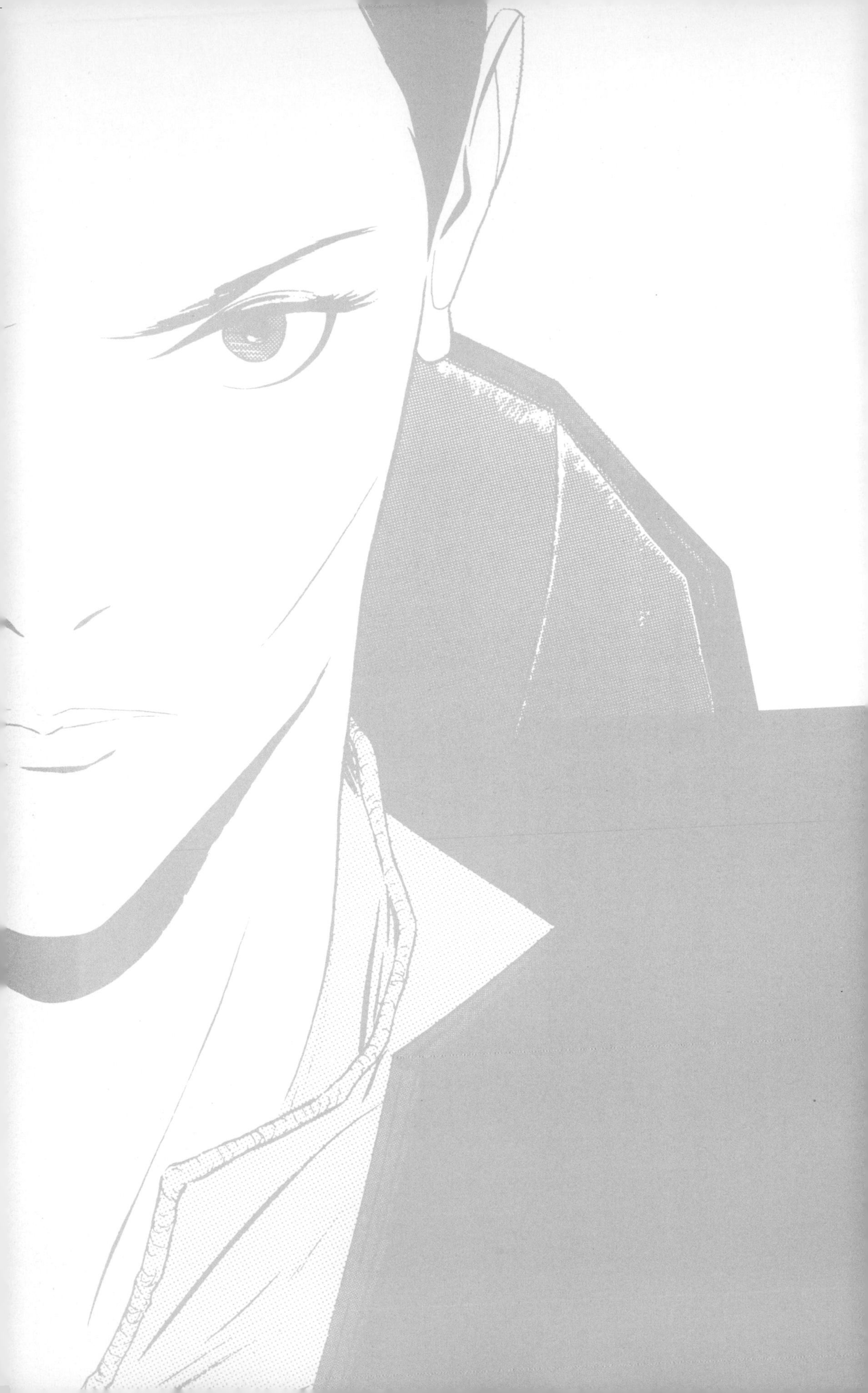

40

 FORTY:
I WILL **SEE YOU**
AGAIN AT THE **END**
OF THE WORLD

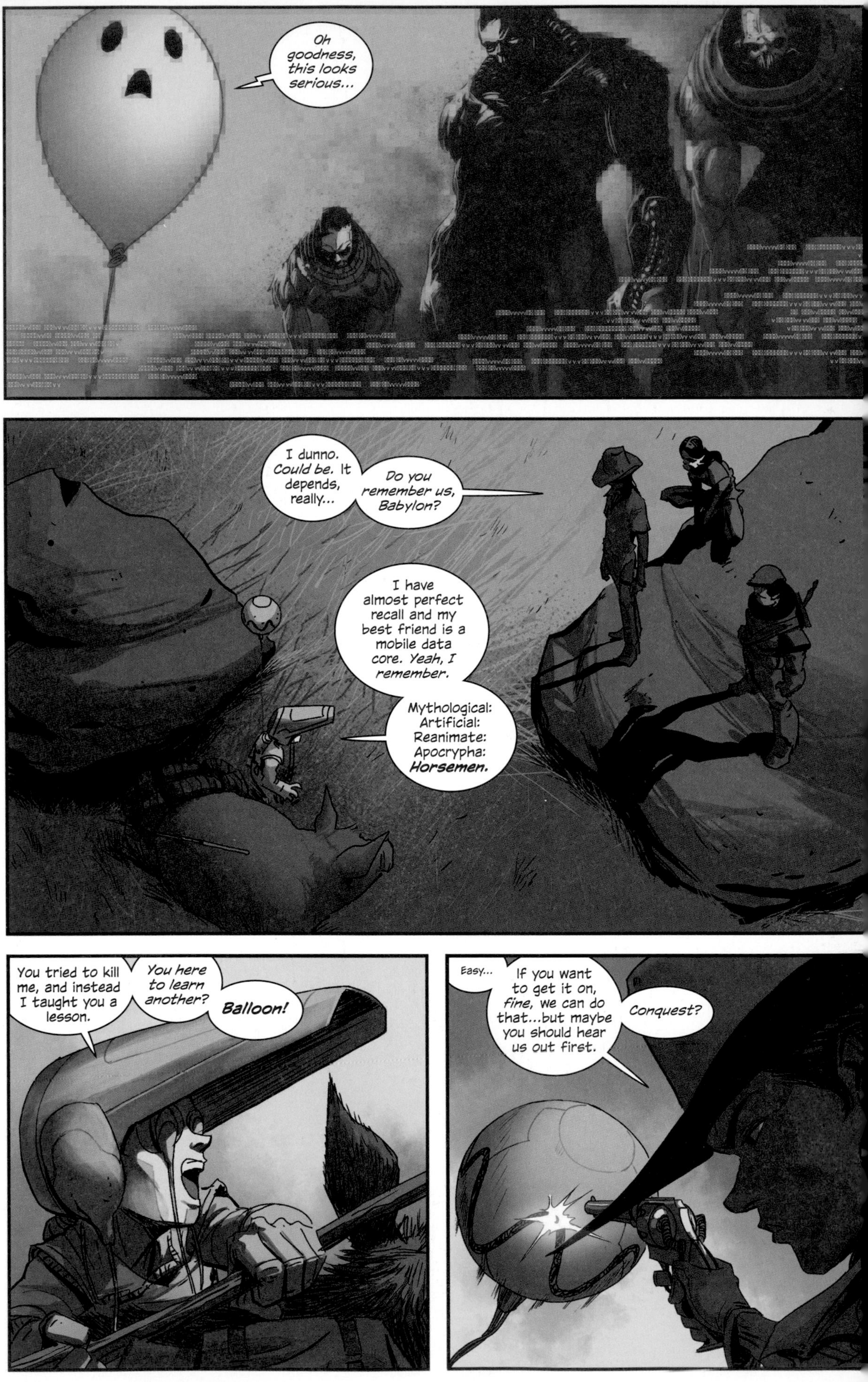
Oh goodness, this looks serious...
I dunno. Could be. It depends, really...
Do you remember us, Babylon?
I have almost perfect recall and my best friend is a mobile data core. Yeah, I remember.
Mythological: Artificial: Reanimate: Apocrypha: Horsemen.
You tried to kill me, and instead I taught you a lesson.
You here to learn another?
Balloon!
Easy...
If you want to get it on, fine, we can do that...but maybe you should hear us out first.
Conquest?

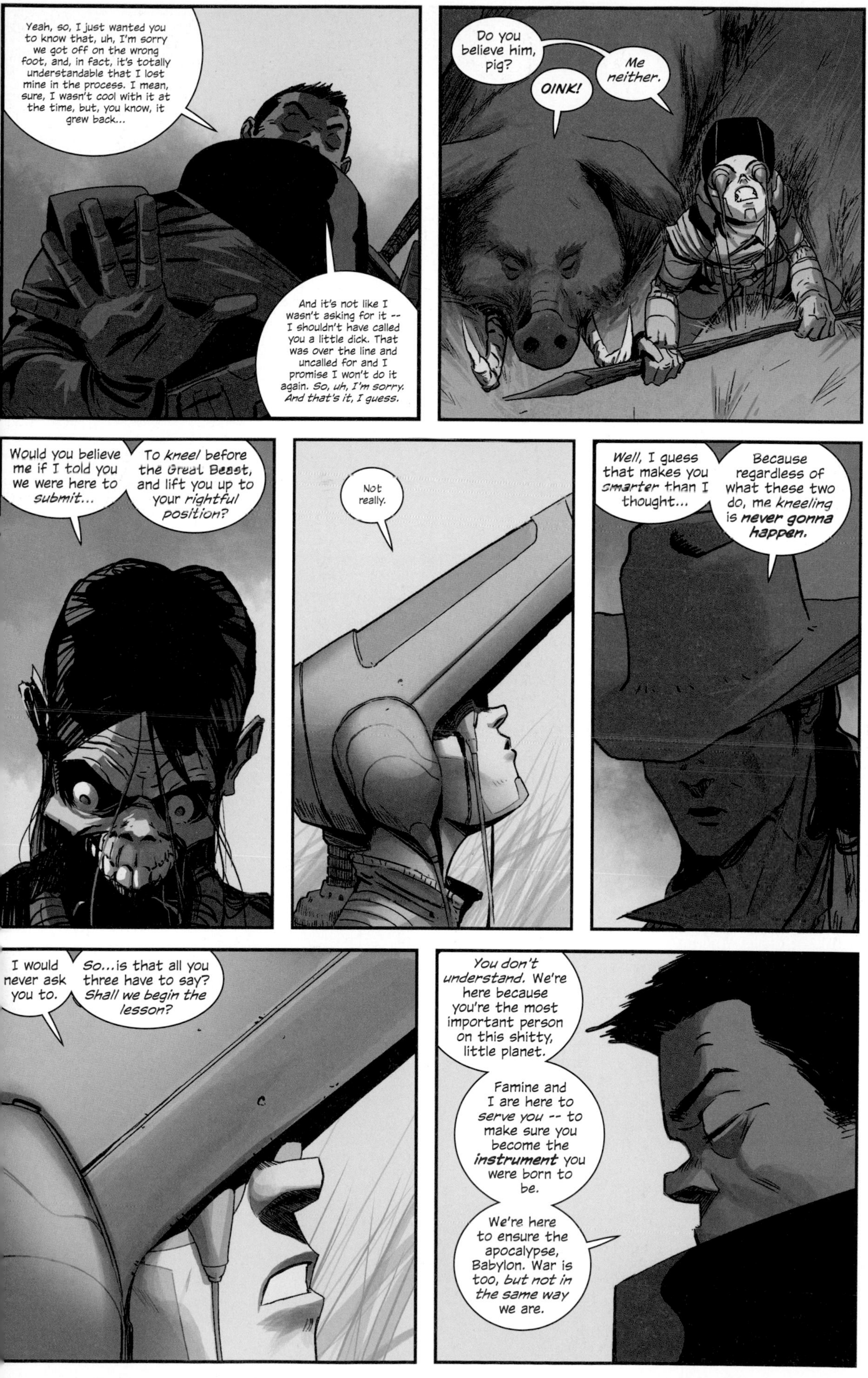
Yeah, so, I just wanted you to know that, uh, I'm sorry we got off on the wrong foot, and, in fact, it's totally understandable that I lost mine in the process. I mean, sure, I wasn't cool with it at the time, but, you know, it grew back...
And it's not like I wasn't asking for it -- I shouldn't have called you a little dick. That was over the line and uncalled for and I promise I won't do it again. So, uh, I'm sorry. And that's it, I guess.
Do you believe him, pig?
OINK!
Me neither.
Would you believe me if I told you we were here to submit...
To kneel before the Great Beast, and lift you up to your rightful position?
Not really.
Well, I guess that makes you smarter than I thought...
Because regardless of what these two do, me kneeling is never gonna happen.
I would never ask you to.
So...is that all you three have to say? Shall we begin the lesson?
You don't understand. We're here because you're the most important person on this shitty, little planet.
Famine and I are here to serve you -- to make sure you become the instrument you were born to be.
We're here to ensure the apocalypse, Babylon. War is too, but not in the same way we are.

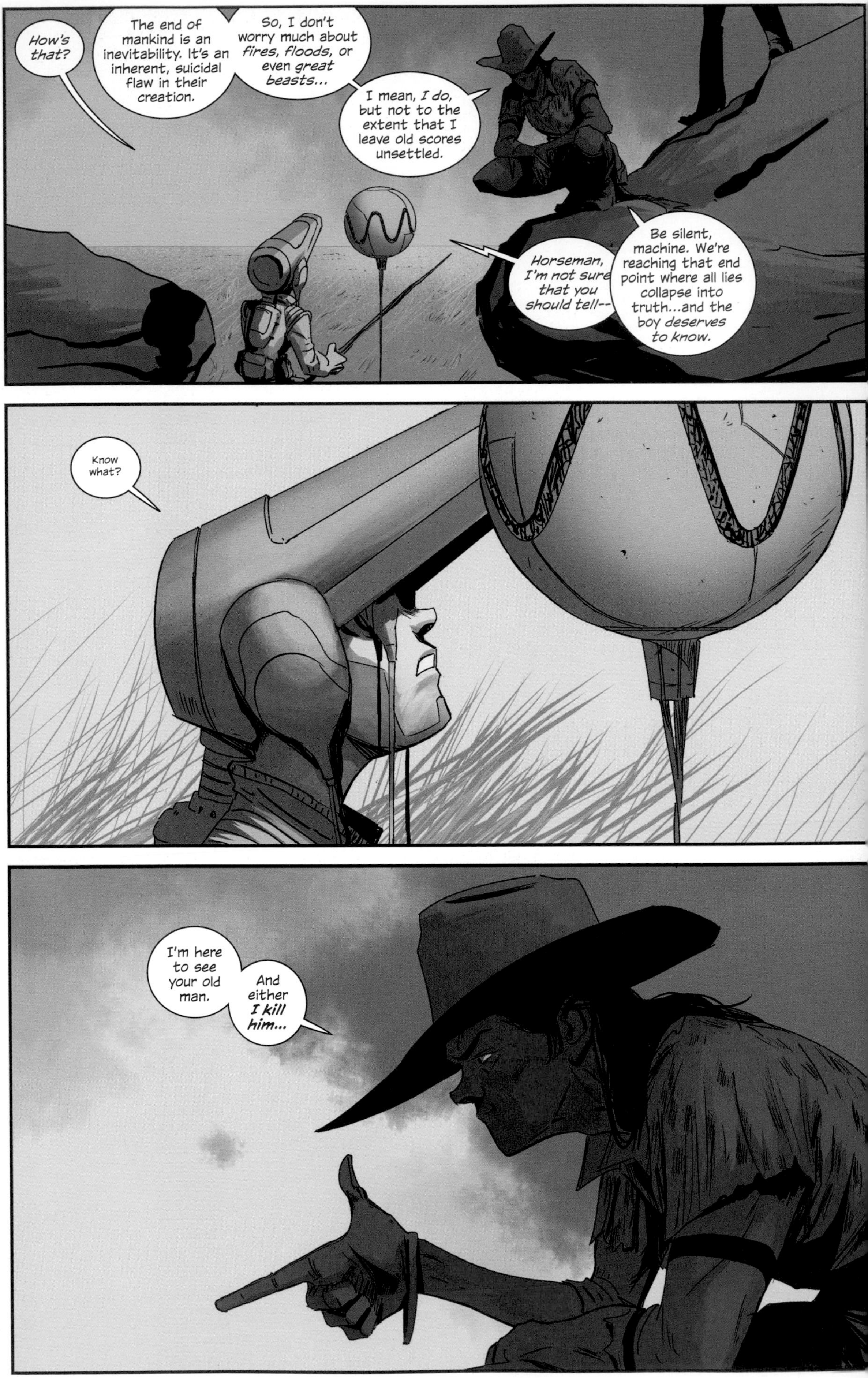
How's that?
The end of mankind is an inevitability. It's an inherent, suicidal flaw in their creation.
So, I don't worry much about fires, floods, or even great beasts...
I mean, I do, but not to the extent that I leave old scores unsettled.
Horseman, I'm not sure that you should tell--
Be silent, machine. We're reaching that end point where all lies collapse into truth...and the boy deserves to know.
Know what?
I'm here to see your old man.
And either I kill him...

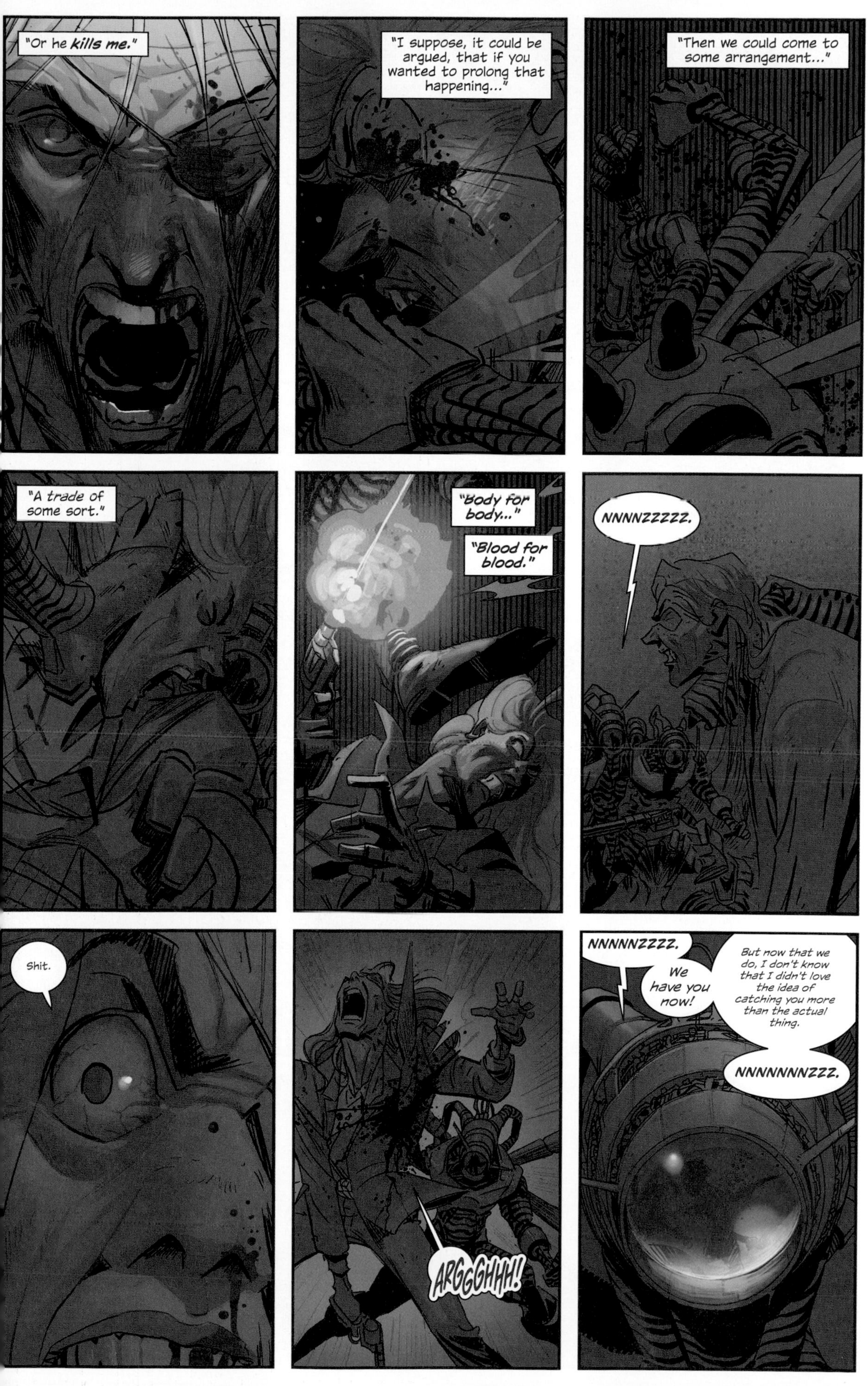
"Or he kills me."
"I suppose, it could be argued, that if you wanted to prolong that happening..."
"Then we could come to some arrangement..."
"A trade of some sort."
"Body for body..."
"Blood for blood."
NNNNZZZZZ.
Shit.
ARGGGHHH!
NNNNNZZZZ.
We have you now!
But now that we do, I don't know that I didn't love the idea of catching you more than the actual thing.
NNNNNNNZZZ.

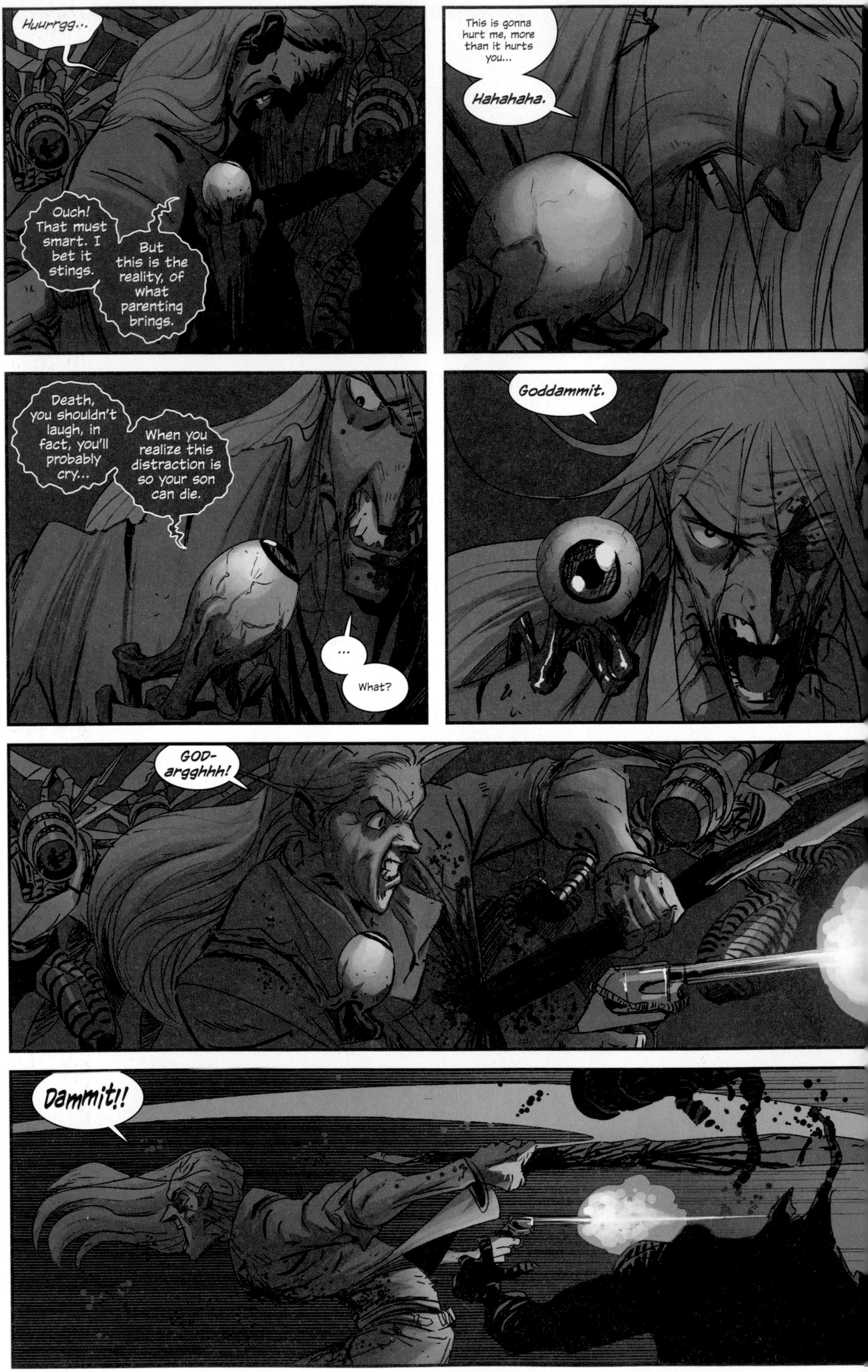

Huurrgg...
Ouch! That must smart. I bet it stings.
But this is the reality, of what parenting brings.
This is gonna hurt me, more than it hurts you...
Hahahaha.
Death, you shouldn't laugh, in fact, you'll probably cry...
When you realize this distraction is so your son can die.
...
What?
Goddammit.
GOD-argghhh!
Dammit!!

RAAARRR!

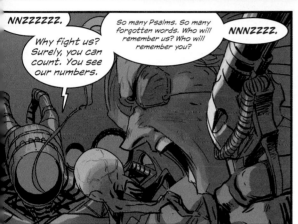

NNZZZZZZ.

Why fight us? Surely, you can count. You see our numbers.

So many Psalms. So many forgotten words. Who will remember us? Who will remember you?

NNNZZZZ.

He has a point. Of them, there are quite a few.

You need a different plan. Maybe get a better view.

Fair enough...

I get your thinkin' -- put a little distance between *yourself* and the *problem*.

See things a bit more clearly.

Well... I see you.
CLICK!
NNZZZZZZ!
NNNZZZZZ!
NNNZZZZZ!
NNZZZZZZ!

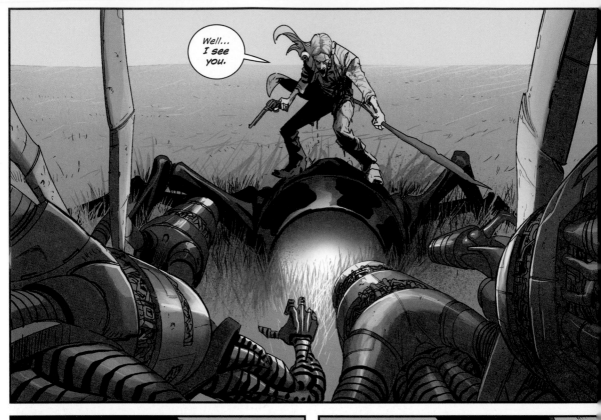

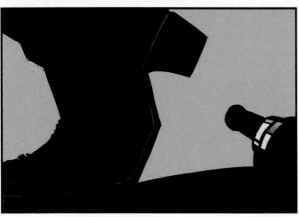

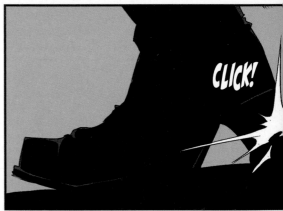

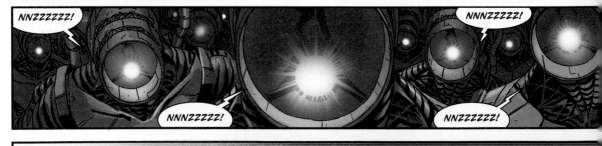

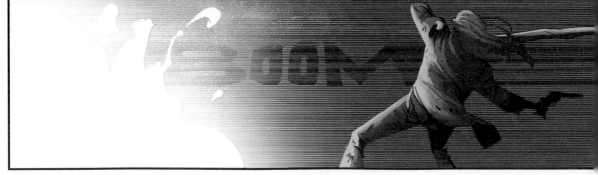

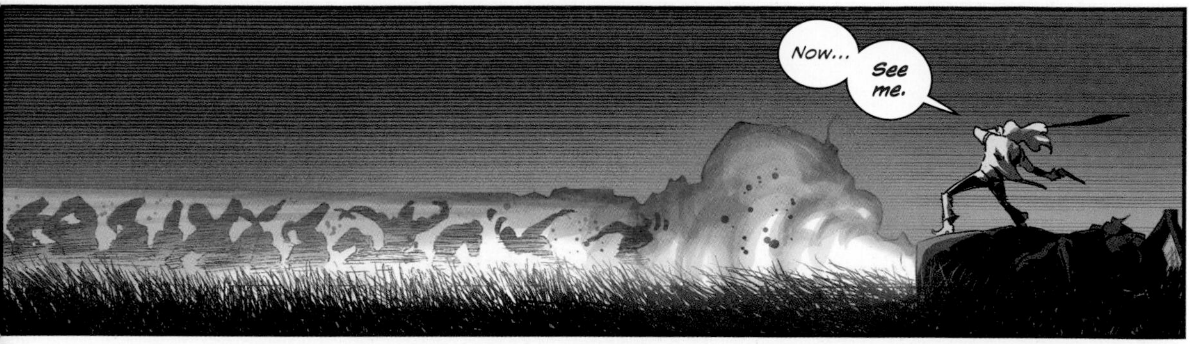
Now...
See me.

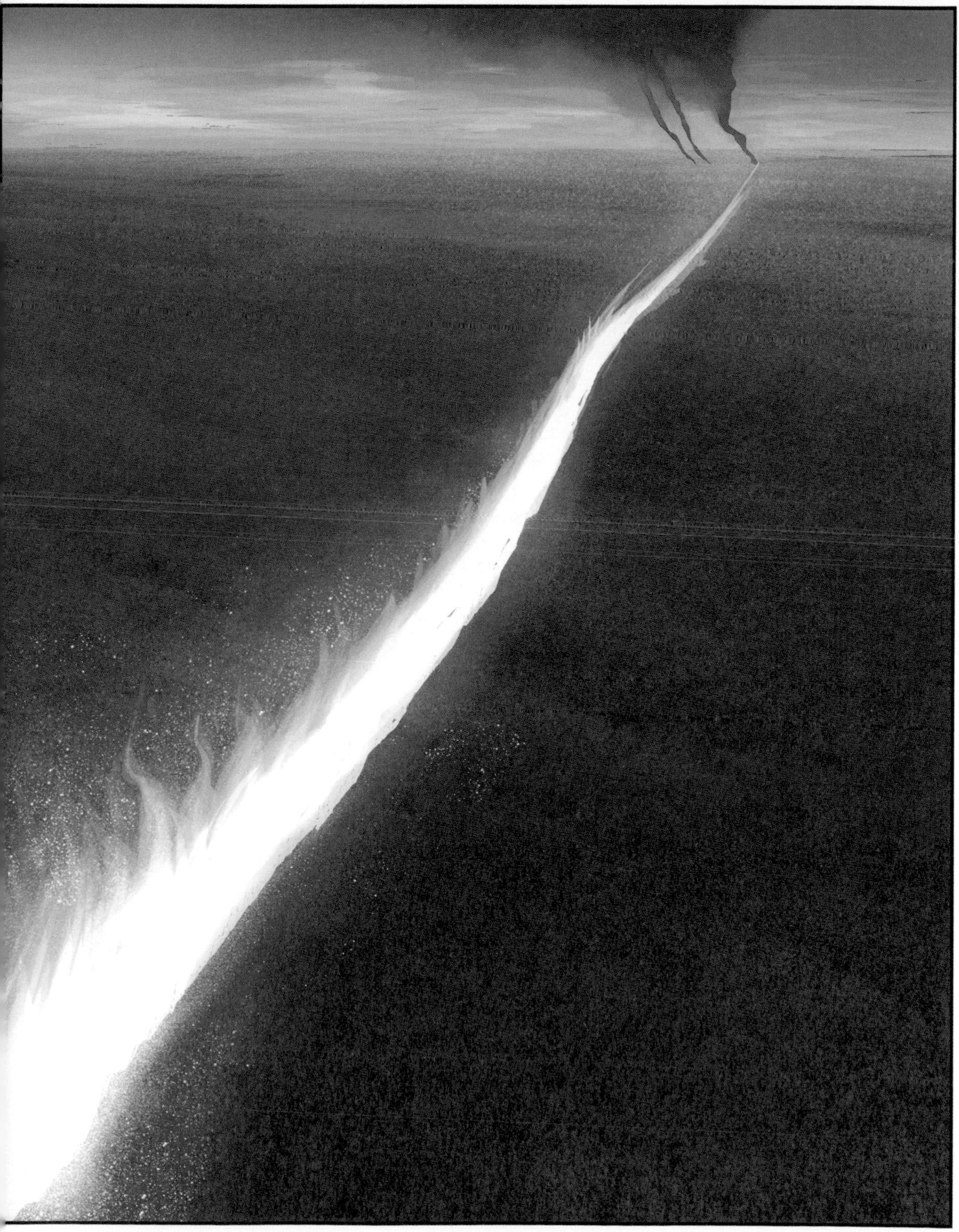

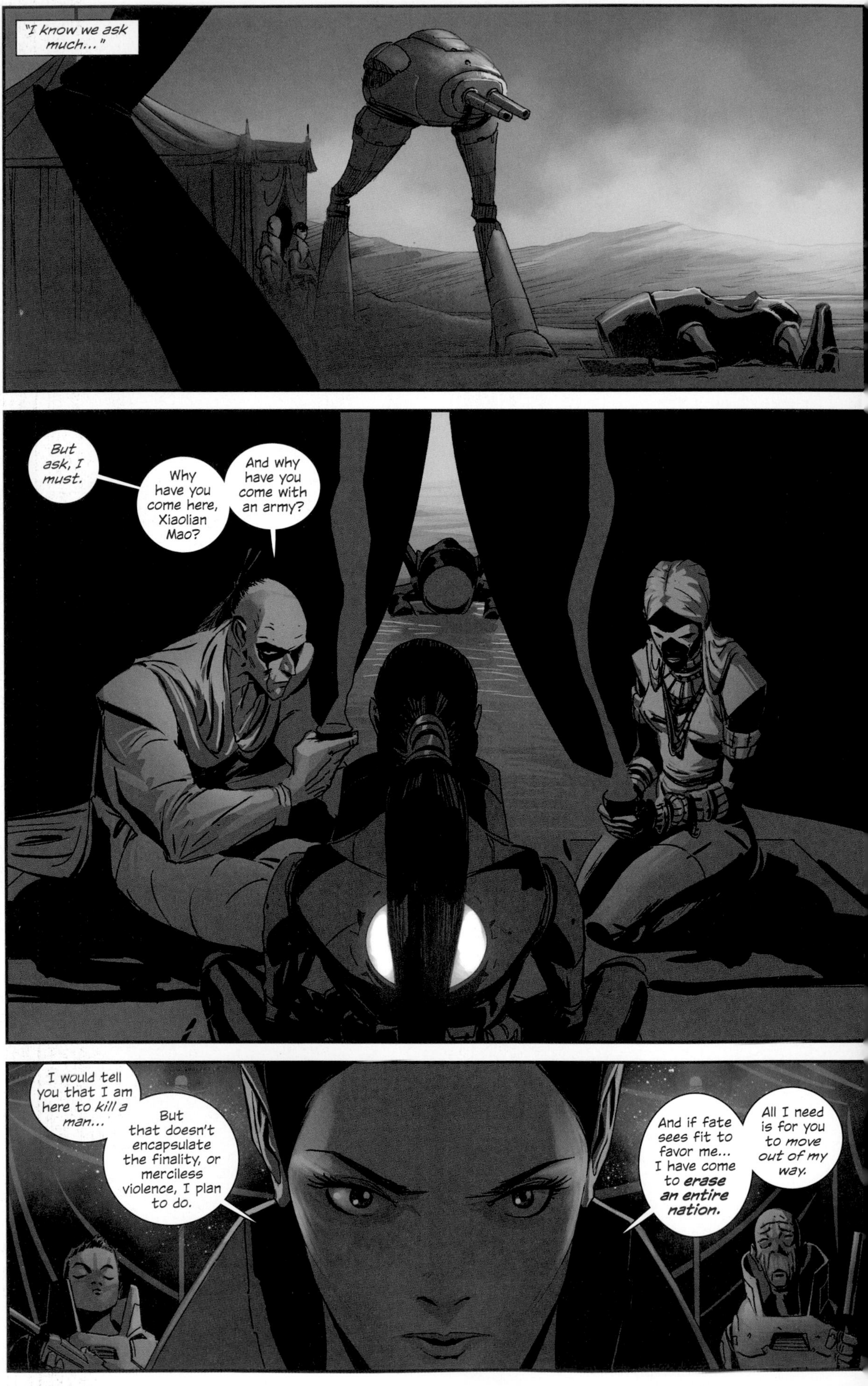
"I know we ask much..."
But ask, I must.
Why have you come here, Xiaolian Mao?
And why have you come with an army?
I would tell you that I am here to *kill a man...*
But that doesn't encapsulate the finality, or merciless violence, I plan to do.
And if fate sees fit to favor me... I have come to ***erase an entire nation.***
All I need is for you to *move out of my way.*

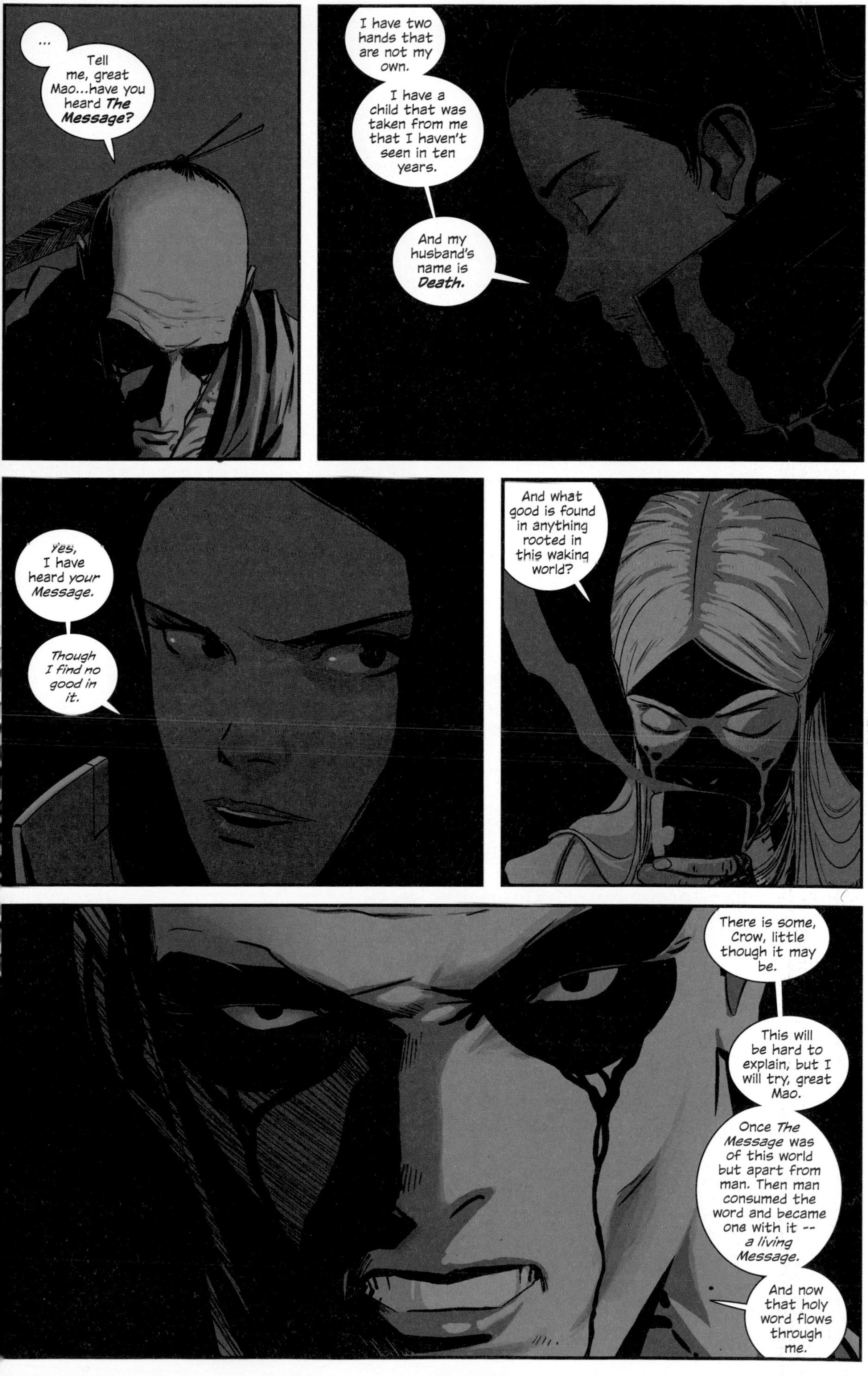
...
Tell me, great Mao...have you heard *The Message?*
I have two hands that are not my own.
I have a child that was taken from me that I haven't seen in ten years.
And my husband's name is *Death.*
Yes, I have heard *your Message.*
Though I find no good in it.
And what good is found in anything rooted in this waking world?
There is some, Crow, little though it may be.
This will be hard to explain, but I will try, great Mao.
Once *The Message* was of this world but apart from man. Then man consumed the word and became one with it -- *a living Message.*
And now that holy word flows through me.

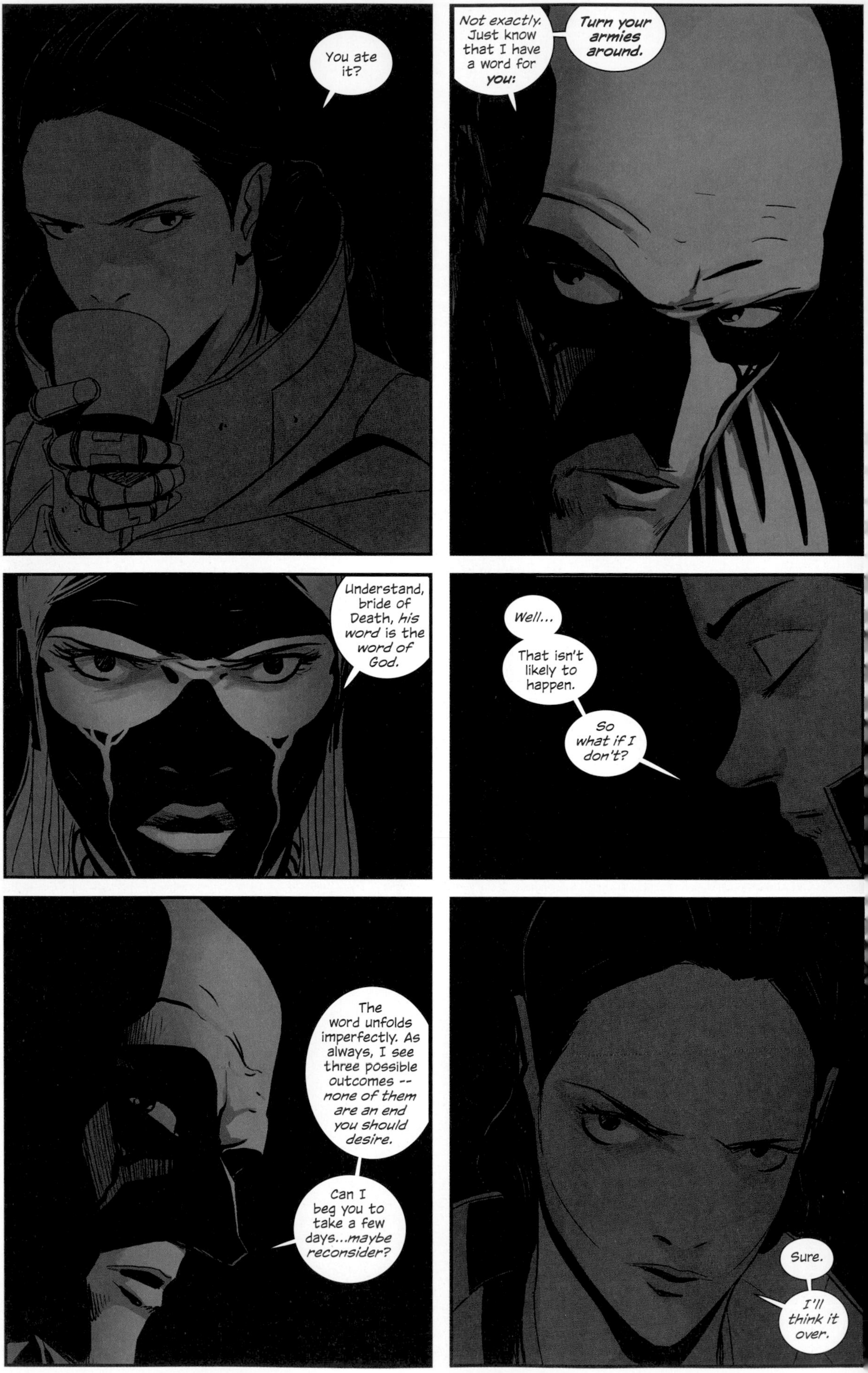
You ate it?
Not exactly. Just know that I have a word for *you:*
Turn your armies around.
Understand, bride of Death, *his word* is the *word of God.*
Well...
That isn't likely to happen.
So what if I don't?
The word unfolds imperfectly. As always, I see three possible outcomes -- *none of them are an end you should desire.*
Can I beg you to take a few days...*maybe reconsider?*
Sure.
I'll think it over.

NNNZZZZZ.

NNZZZZZ. You've destroyed the entire flock. I am the last Psalm. The last remnant of the Remnant.

I wonder what comes next. Do you know if there's something wonderful waiting out there -- beyond the veil?

NNZZZZZ.

I know there is... Just not for you, you son of a bitch.

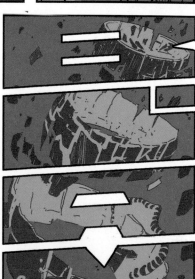

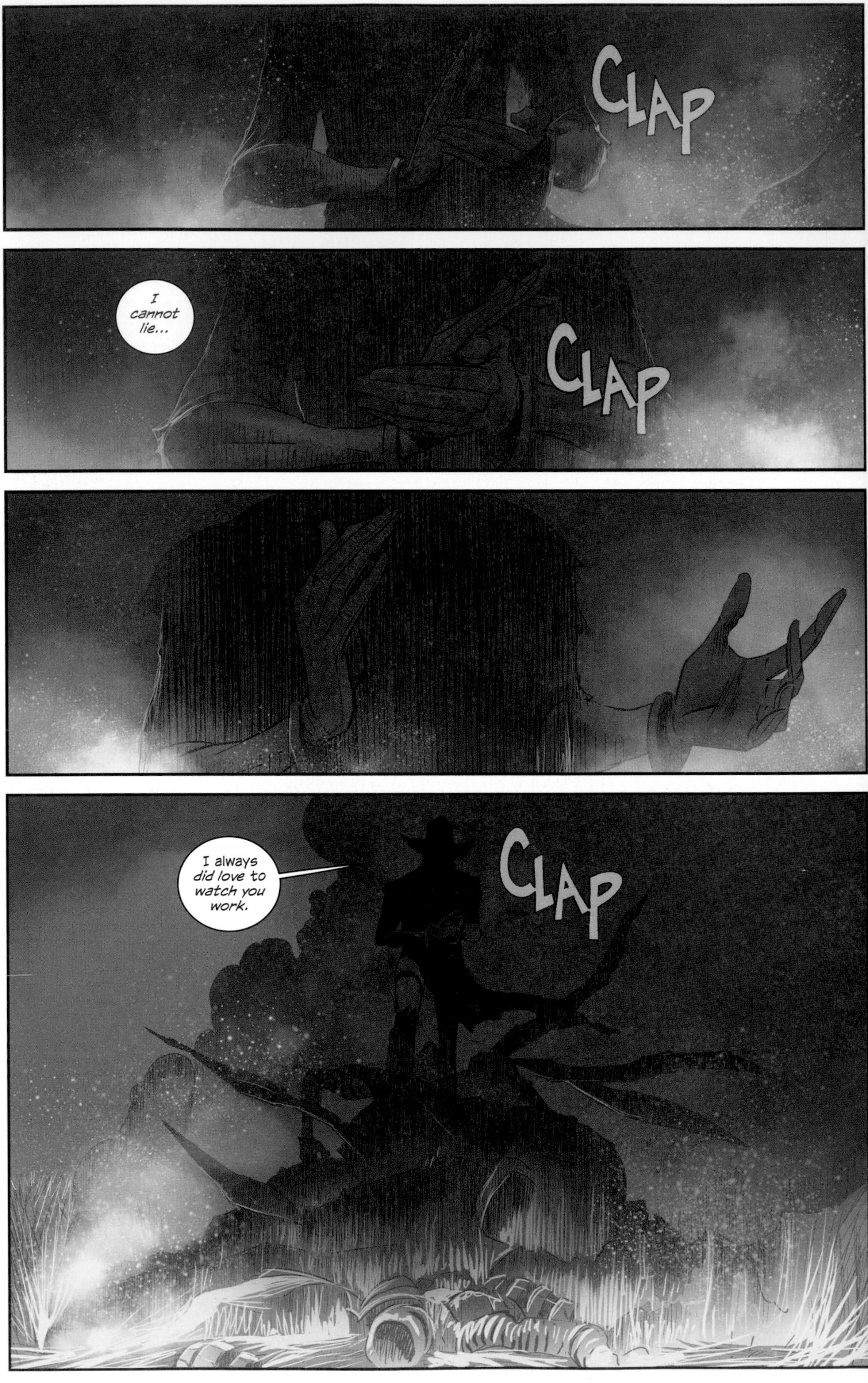
CLAP
I cannot lie...
CLAP
I always did love to watch you work.
CLAP

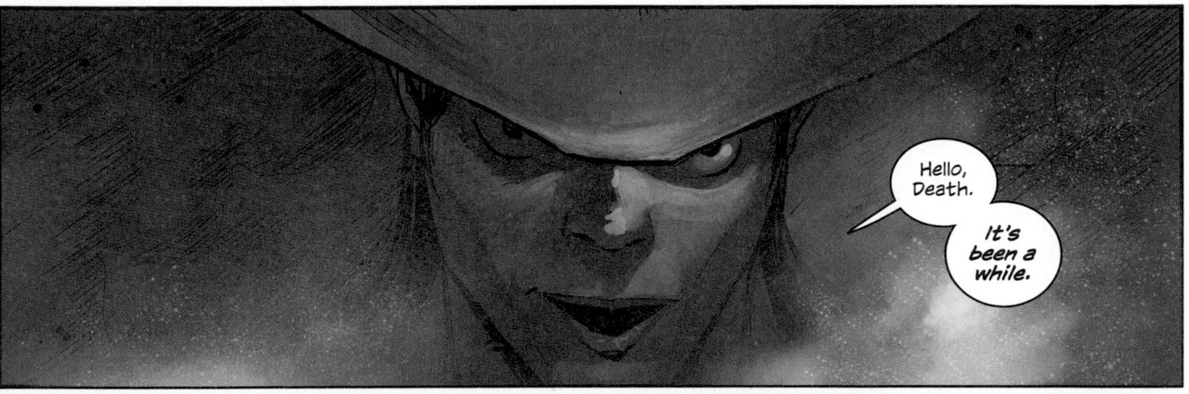
Hello, Death.
It's been a while.
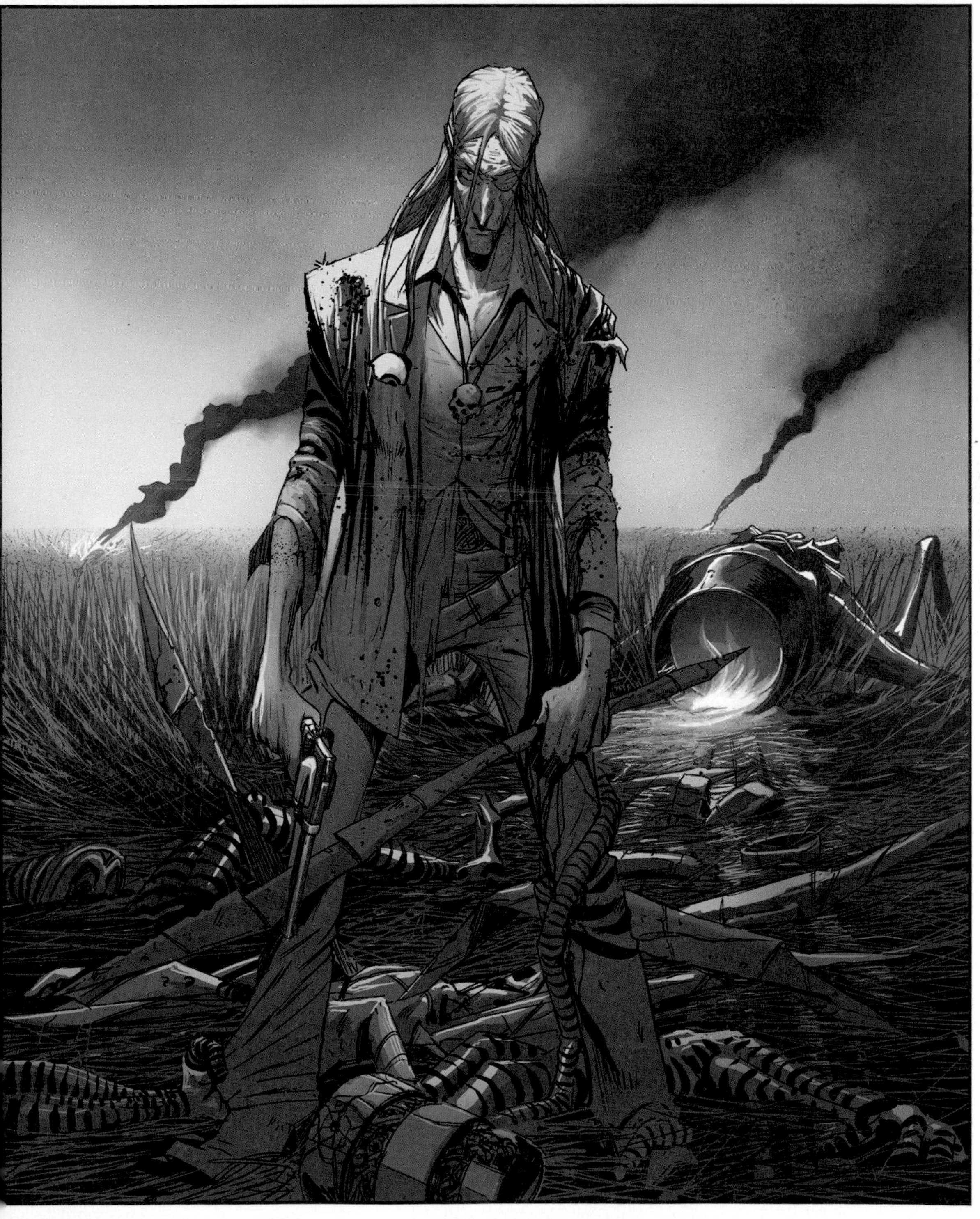

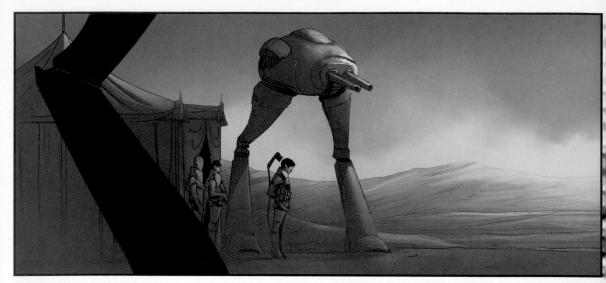

If we're going to be staying here a few days, Premier Mao, we should push our scouts out further than normal. There are provision issues we mig--

There won't be any need for that, General.

But you told them--

I know what I said...

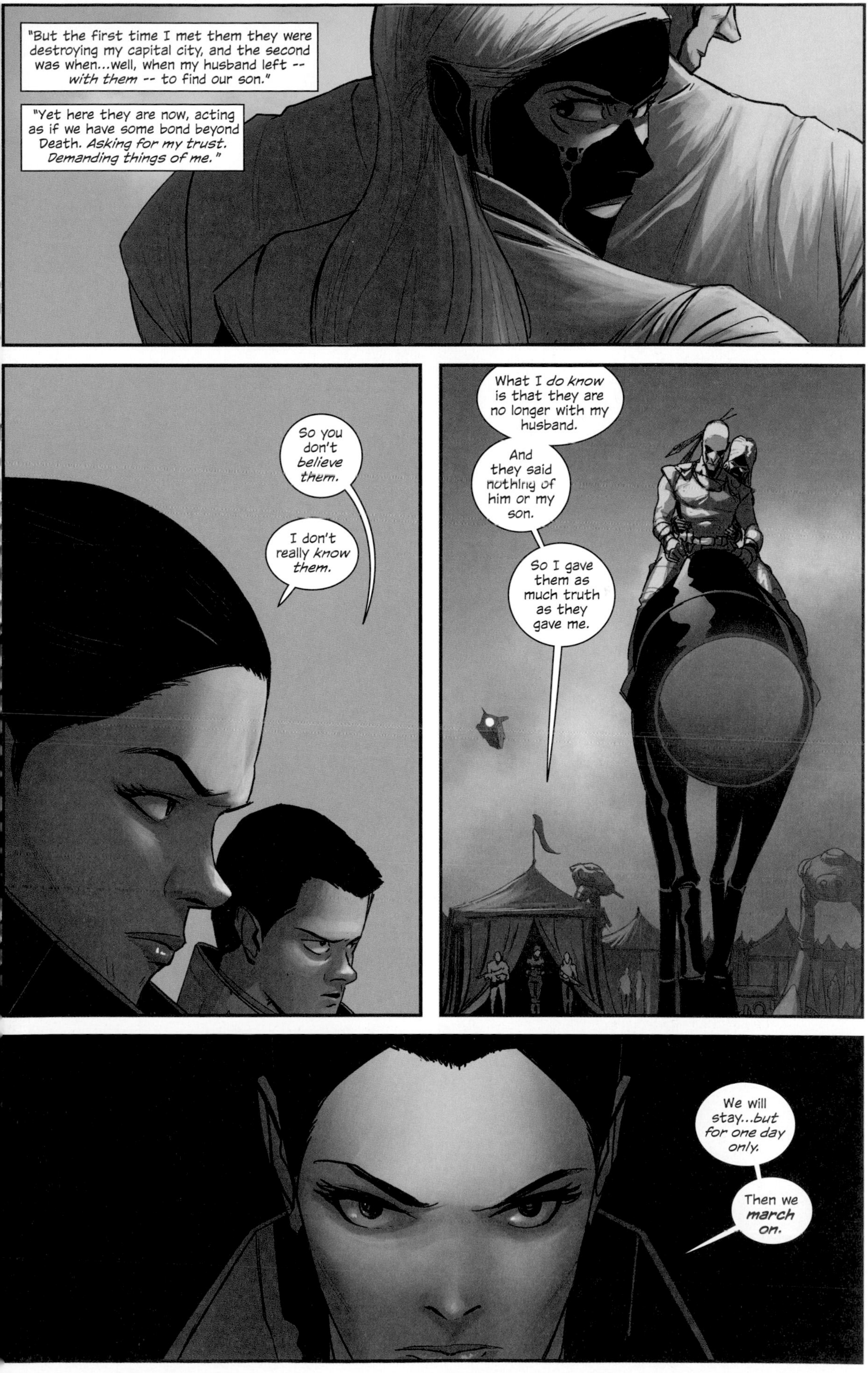
"But the first time I met them they were destroying my capital city, and the second was when...well, when my husband left -- *with them* -- to find our son."
"Yet here they are now, acting as if we have some bond beyond Death. *Asking for my trust. Demanding things of me.*"
So you don't *believe them.*
I don't really *know* them.
What I *do know* is that they are no longer with my husband.
And they said nothing of him or my son.
So I gave them as much truth as they gave me.
We will stay...*but for one day only.*
Then we ***march on.***

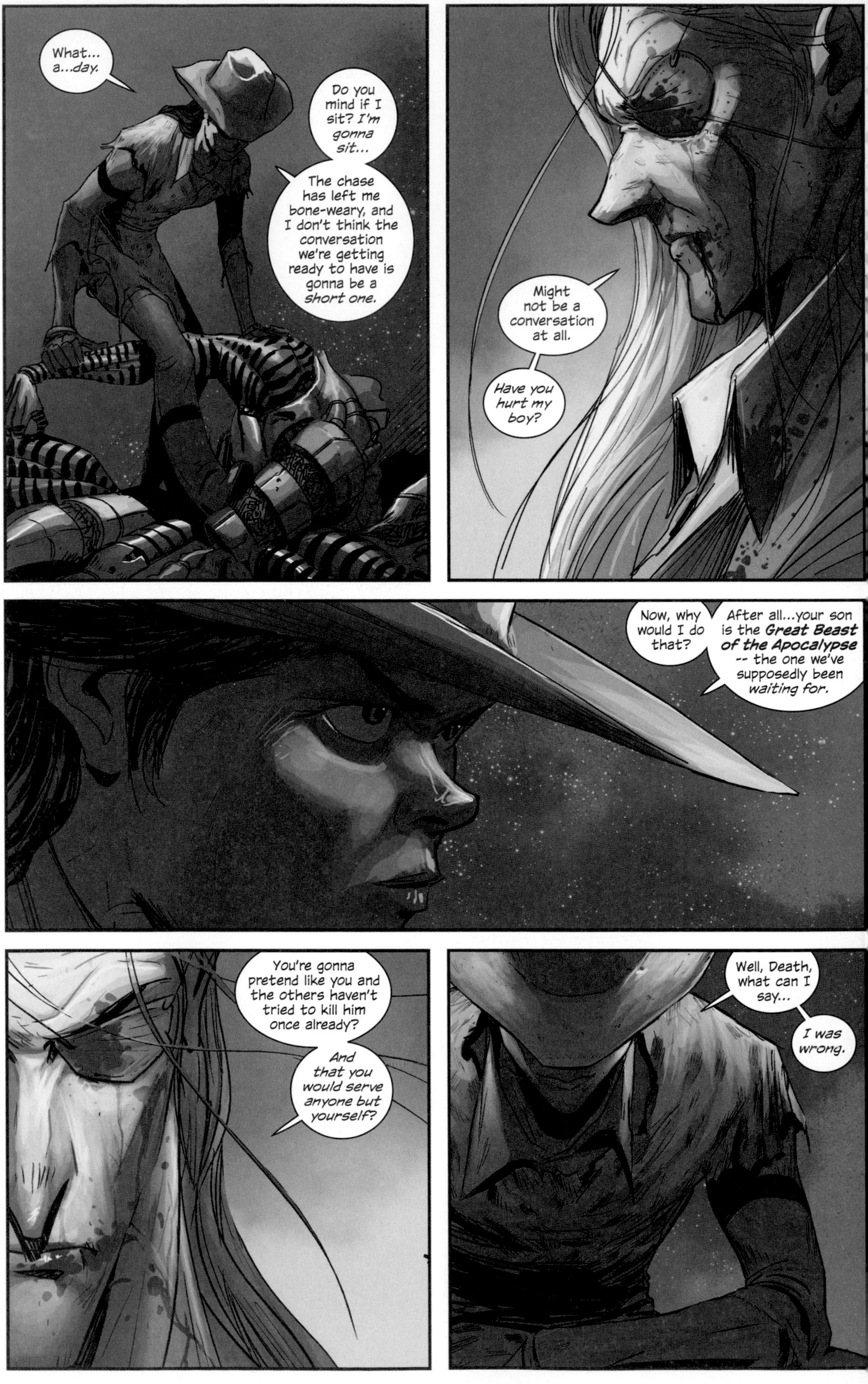
What... a...day.
Do you mind if I sit? I'm gonna sit...
The chase has left me bone-weary, and I don't think the conversation we're getting ready to have is gonna be a short one.
Might not be a conversation at all.
Have you hurt my boy?
Now, why would I do that?
After all...your son is the Great Beast of the Apocalypse -- the one we've supposedly been waiting for.
You're gonna pretend like you and the others haven't tried to kill him once already?
And that you would serve anyone but yourself?
Well, Death, what can I say...
I was wrong.

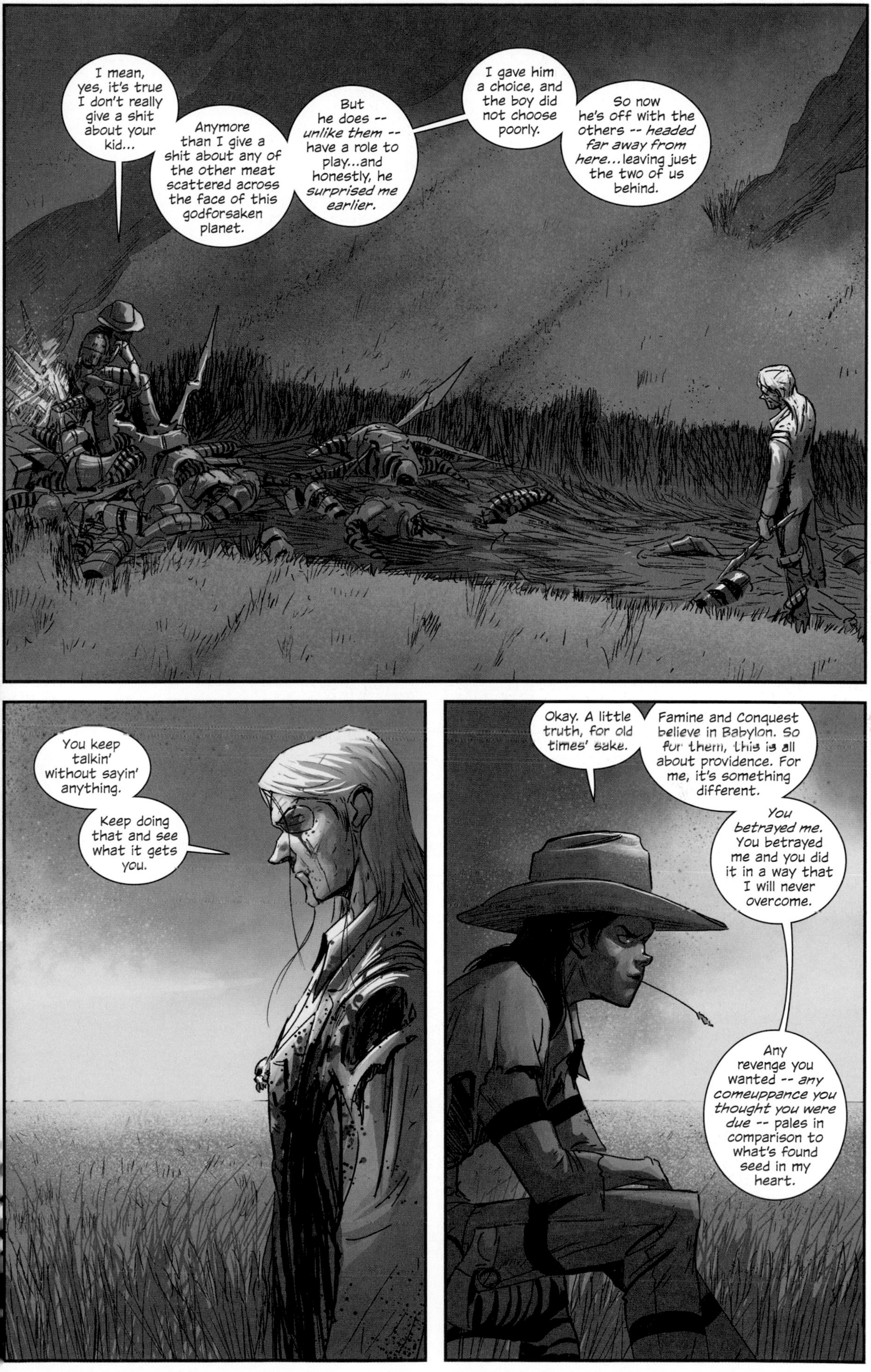
I mean, yes, it's true I don't really give a shit about your kid...
Anymore than I give a shit about any of the other meat scattered across the face of this godforsaken planet.
But he does -- *unlike them* -- have a role to play...and honestly, he *surprised me earlier.*
I gave him a choice, and the boy did not choose poorly.
So now he's off with the others -- *headed far away from here...* leaving just the two of us behind.
You keep talkin' without sayin' anything.
Keep doing that and see what it gets you.
Okay. A little truth, for old times' sake.
Famine and Conquest believe in Babylon. So for them, this is all about providence. For me, it's something different.
You betrayed me. You betrayed me and you did it in a way that I will never overcome.
Any revenge you wanted -- *any comeuppance you thought you were due* -- pales in comparison to what's found seed in my heart.

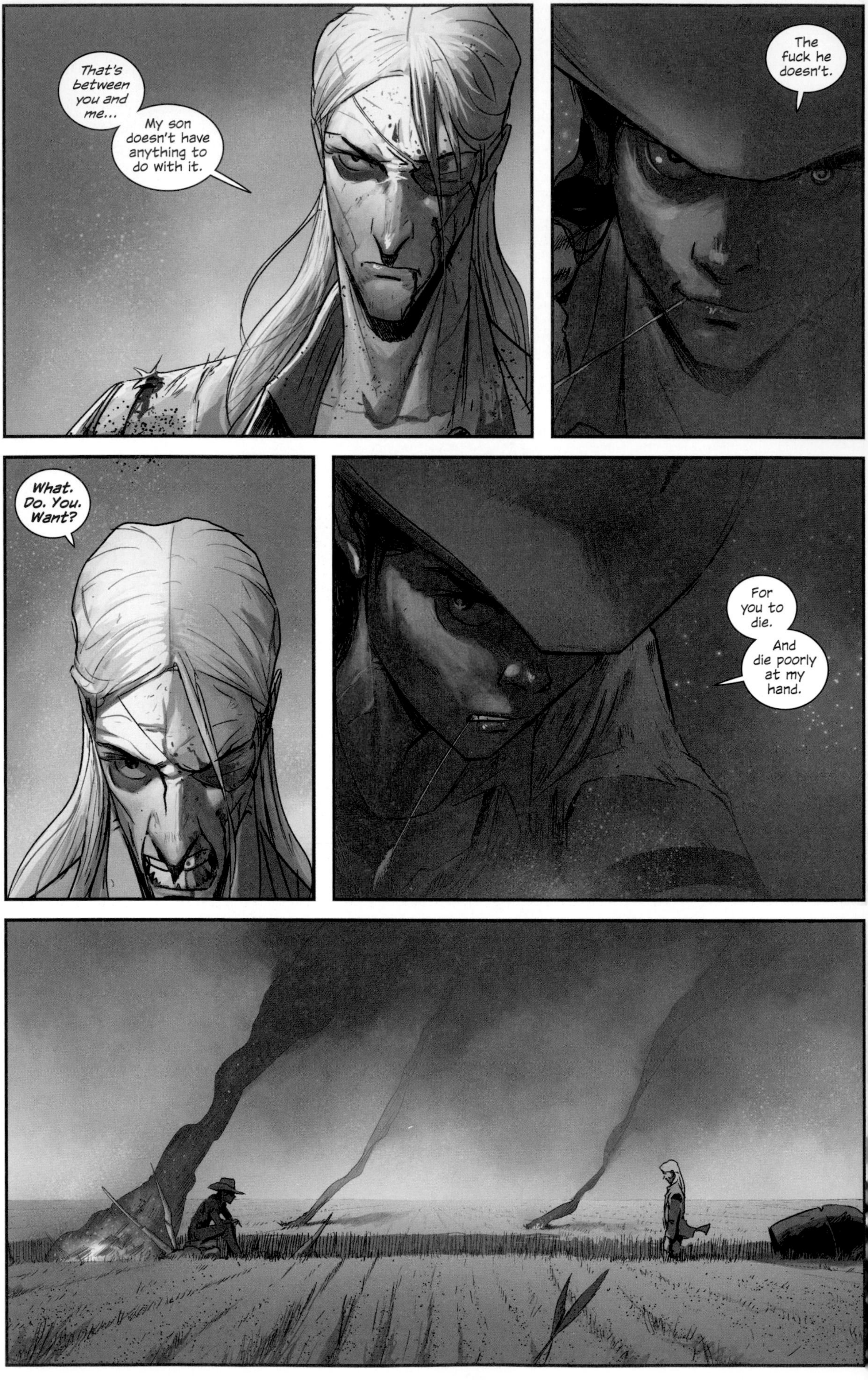
That's between you and me...
My son doesn't have anything to do with it.
The fuck he doesn't.
What. Do. You. Want?
For you to die.
And die poorly at my hand.

So, how's that sound?

...

Fair enough. *Fine.*

Just let the boy go.

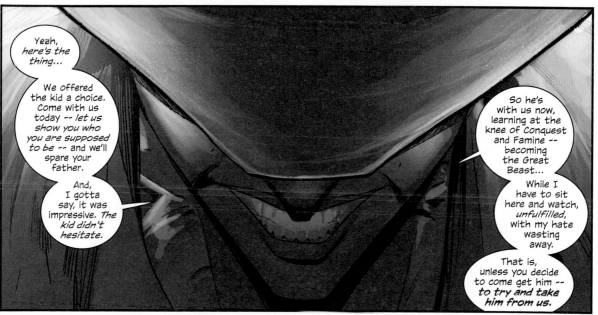

Yeah, here's the thing...

We offered the kid a choice. Come with us today -- let us show you who you are supposed to be -- and we'll spare your father.

And, I gotta say, it was impressive. *The kid didn't hesitate.*

So he's with us now, learning at the knee of Conquest and Famine -- becoming the Great Beast...

While I have to sit here and watch, *unfulfilled*, with my hate wasting away.

That is, unless you decide to come get him -- *to try and take him from us.*

CLICK!

Oh, I'm comin' -- you can count on that.

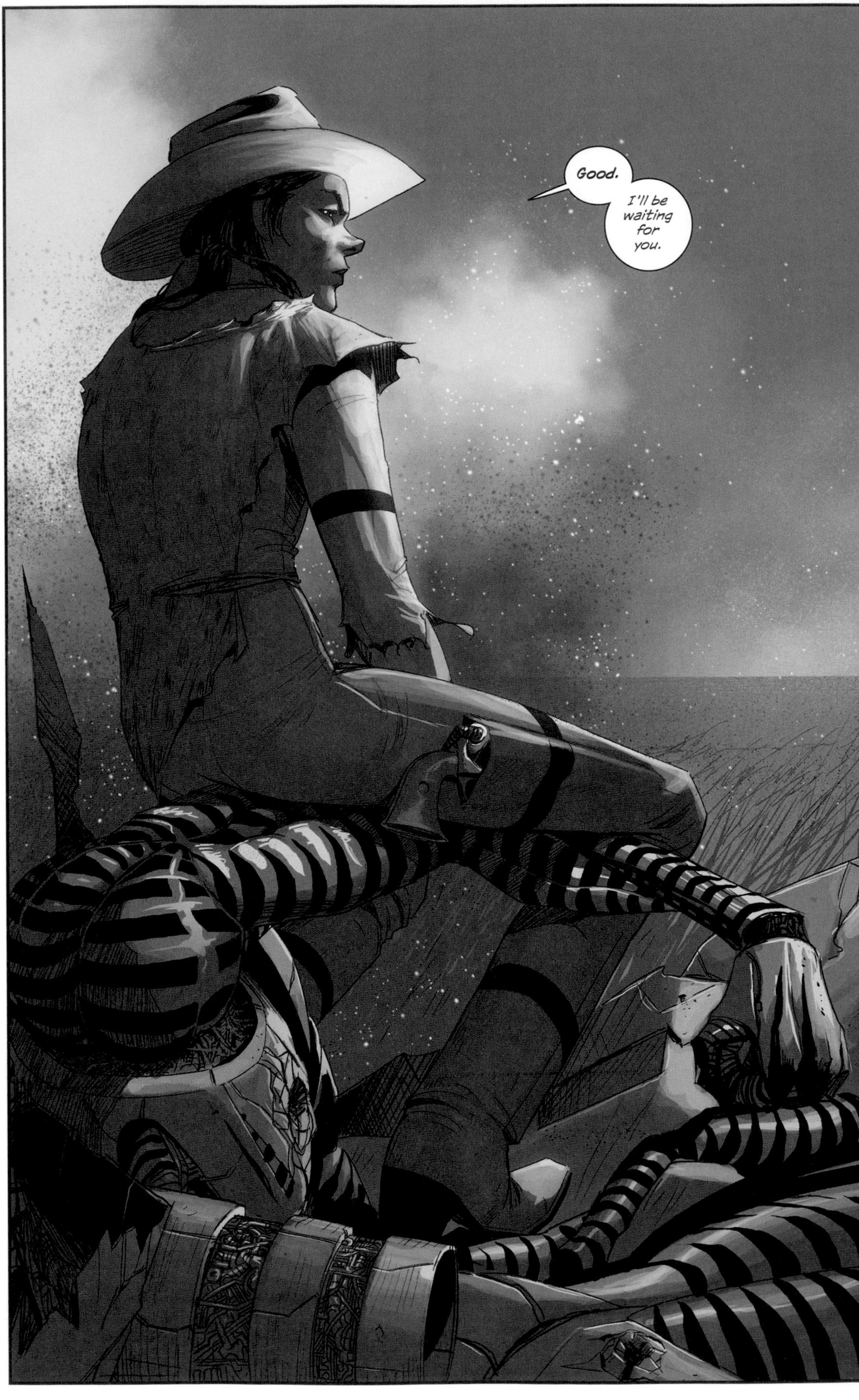
Good.
I'll be waiting for you.

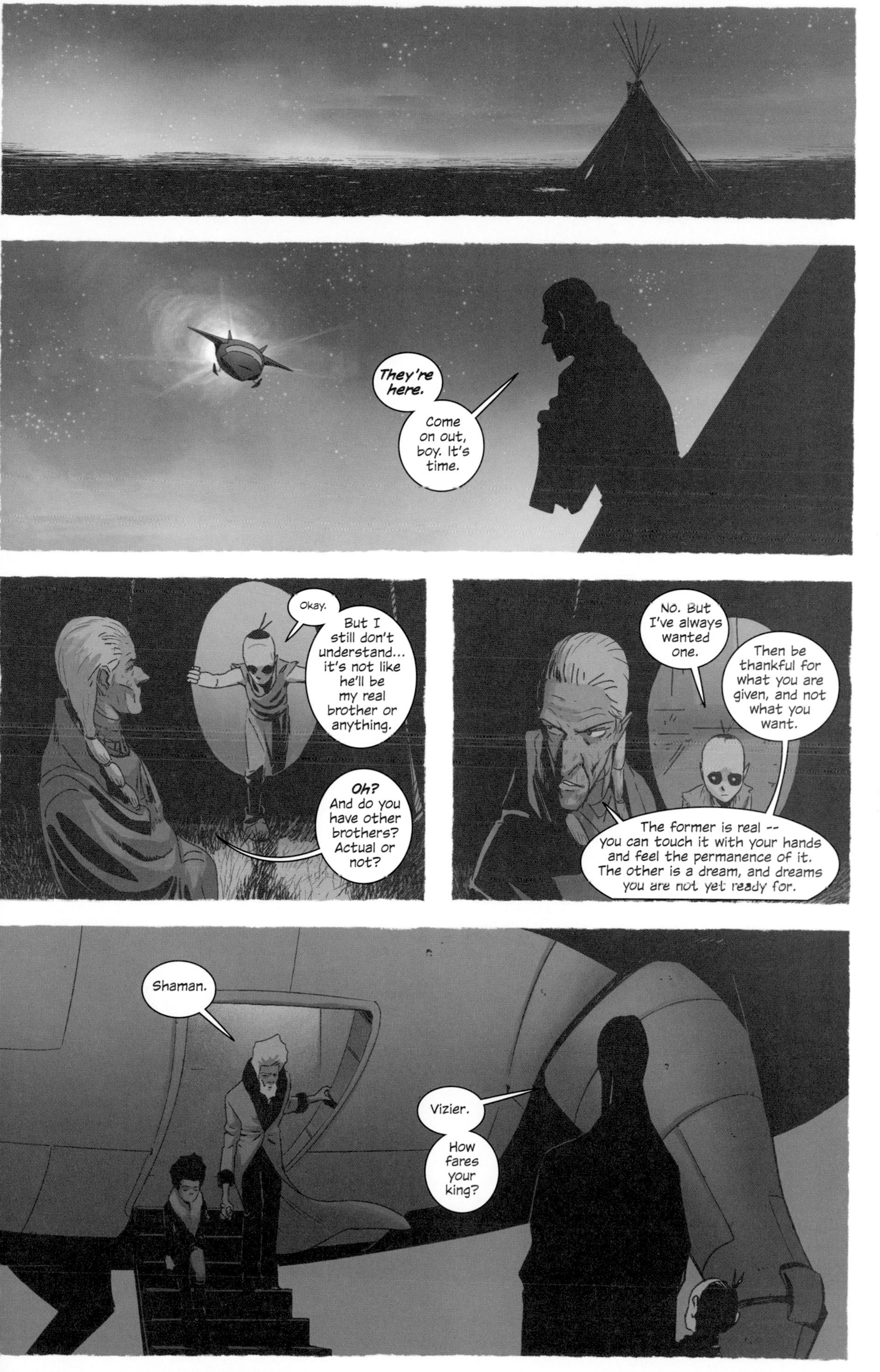
They're here.
Come on out, boy. It's time.
Okay.
But I still don't understand... it's not like he'll be my real brother or anything.
Oh? And do you have other brothers? Actual or not?
No. But I've always wanted one.
Then be thankful for what you are given, and not what you want.
The former is real -- you can touch it with your hands and feel the permanence of it. The other is a dream, and dreams you are not yet ready for.
Shaman.
Vizier.
How fares your king?

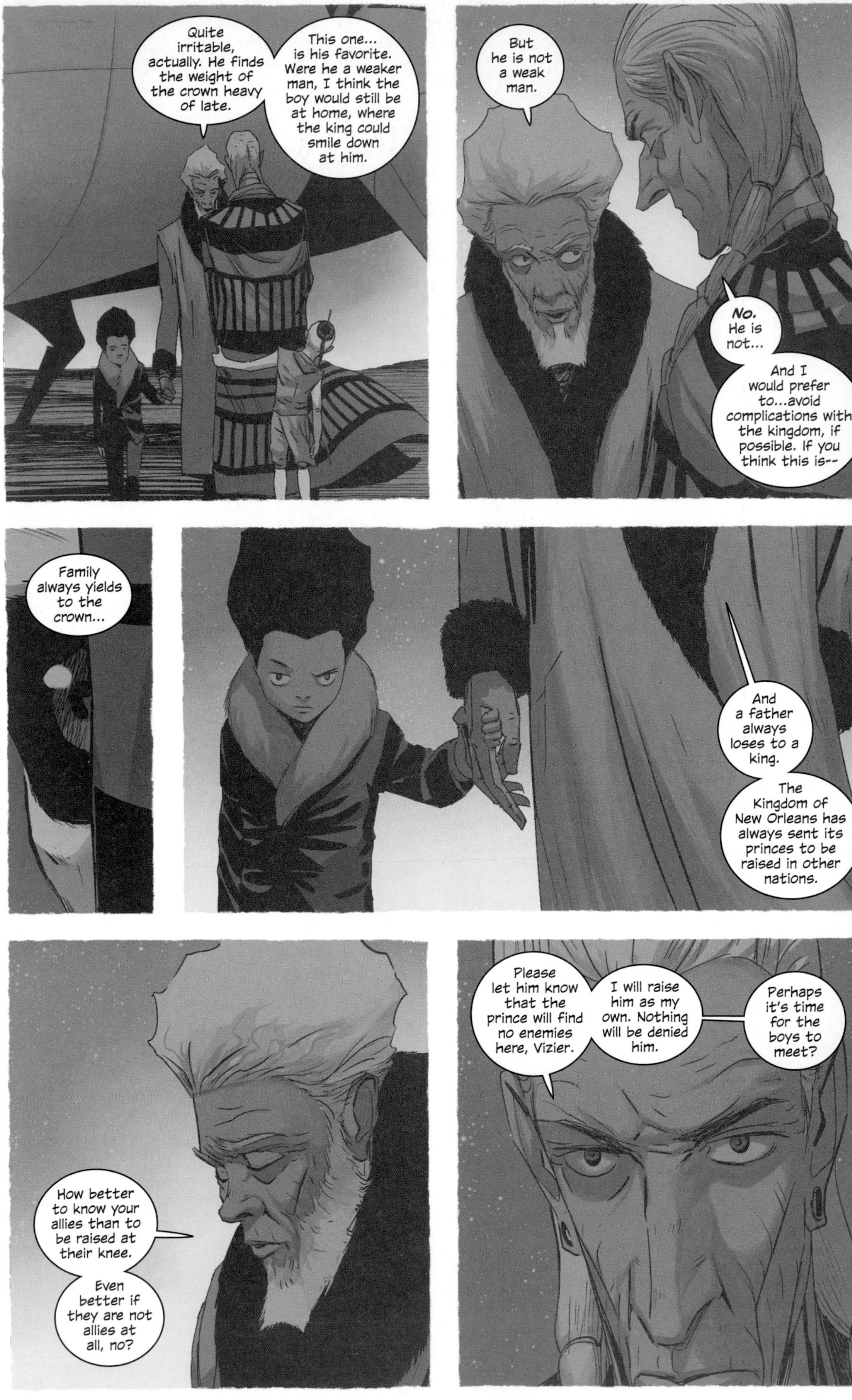
Quite irritable, actually. He finds the weight of the crown heavy of late.
This one... is his favorite. Were he a weaker man, I think the boy would still be at home, where the king could smile down at him.
But he is not a weak man.
No. He is not...
And I would prefer to...avoid complications with the kingdom, if possible. If you think this is--
Family always yields to the crown...
And a father always loses to a king.
The Kingdom of New Orleans has always sent its princes to be raised in other nations.
How better to know your allies than to be raised at their knee.
Even better if they are not allies at all, no?
Please let him know that the prince will find no enemies here, Vizier.
I will raise him as my own. Nothing will be denied him.
Perhaps it's time for the boys to meet?

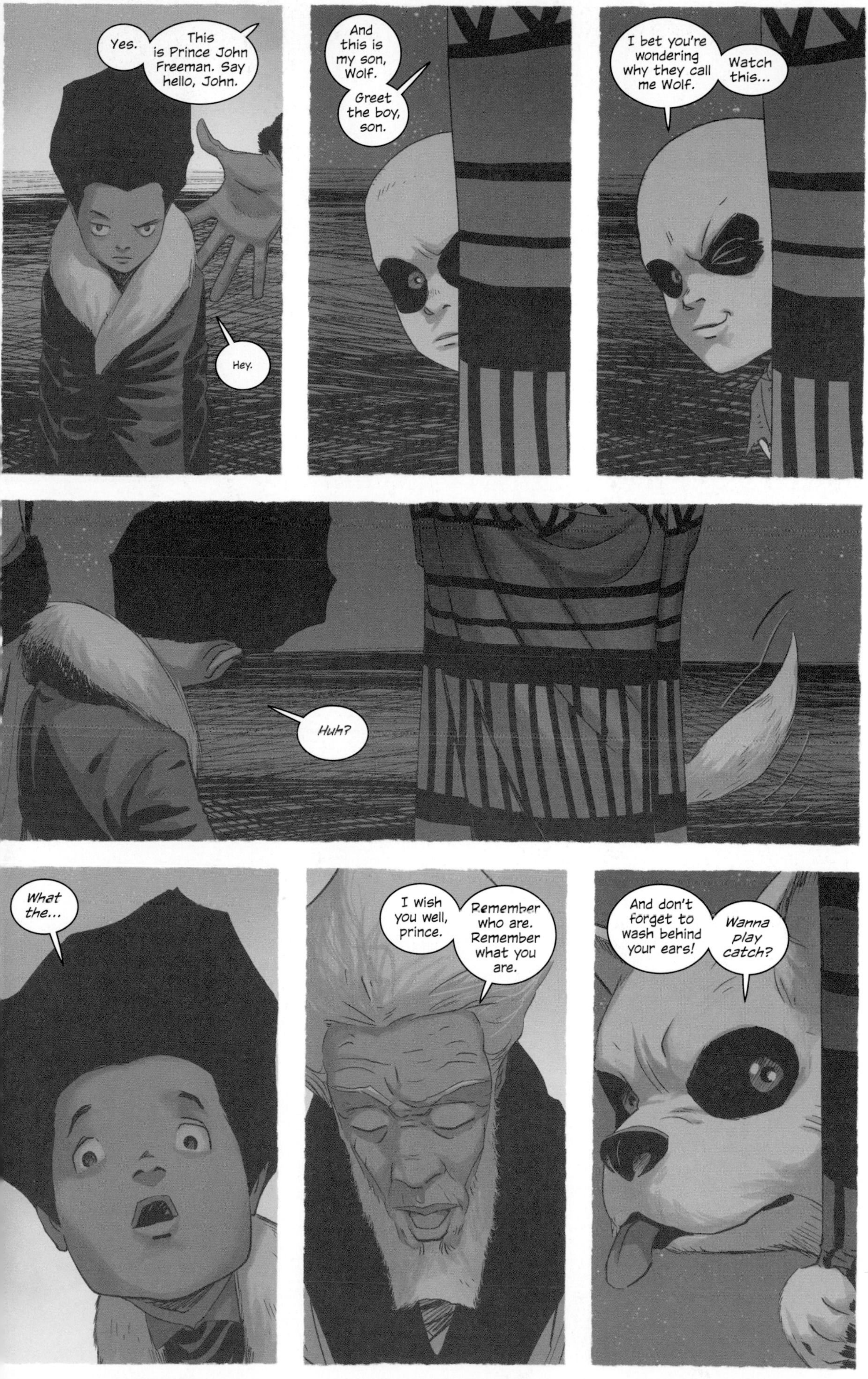
Yes.
This is Prince John Freeman. Say hello, John.
Hey.
And this is my son, Wolf.
Greet the boy, son.
I bet you're wondering why they call me Wolf.
Watch this...
Huh?
What the...
I wish you well, prince.
Remember who are. Remember what you are.
And don't forget to wash behind your ears!
Wanna play catch?

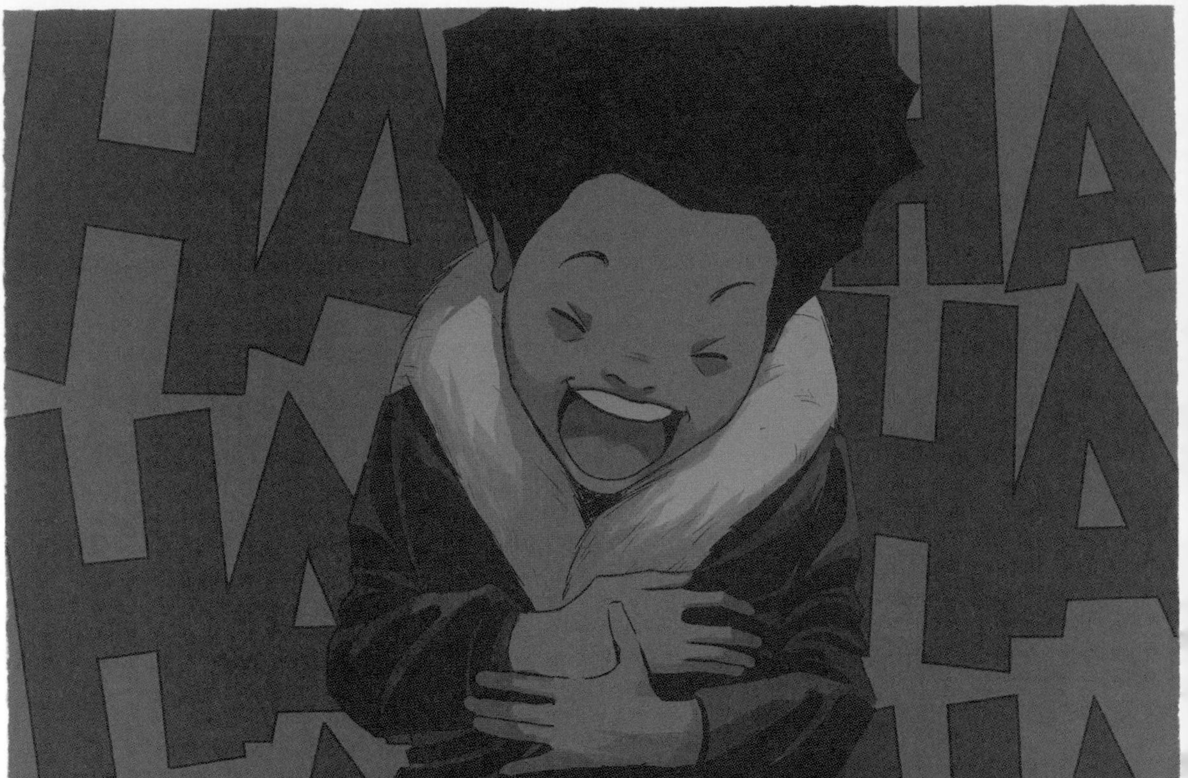
HA HA HA HA HA HA HA HA

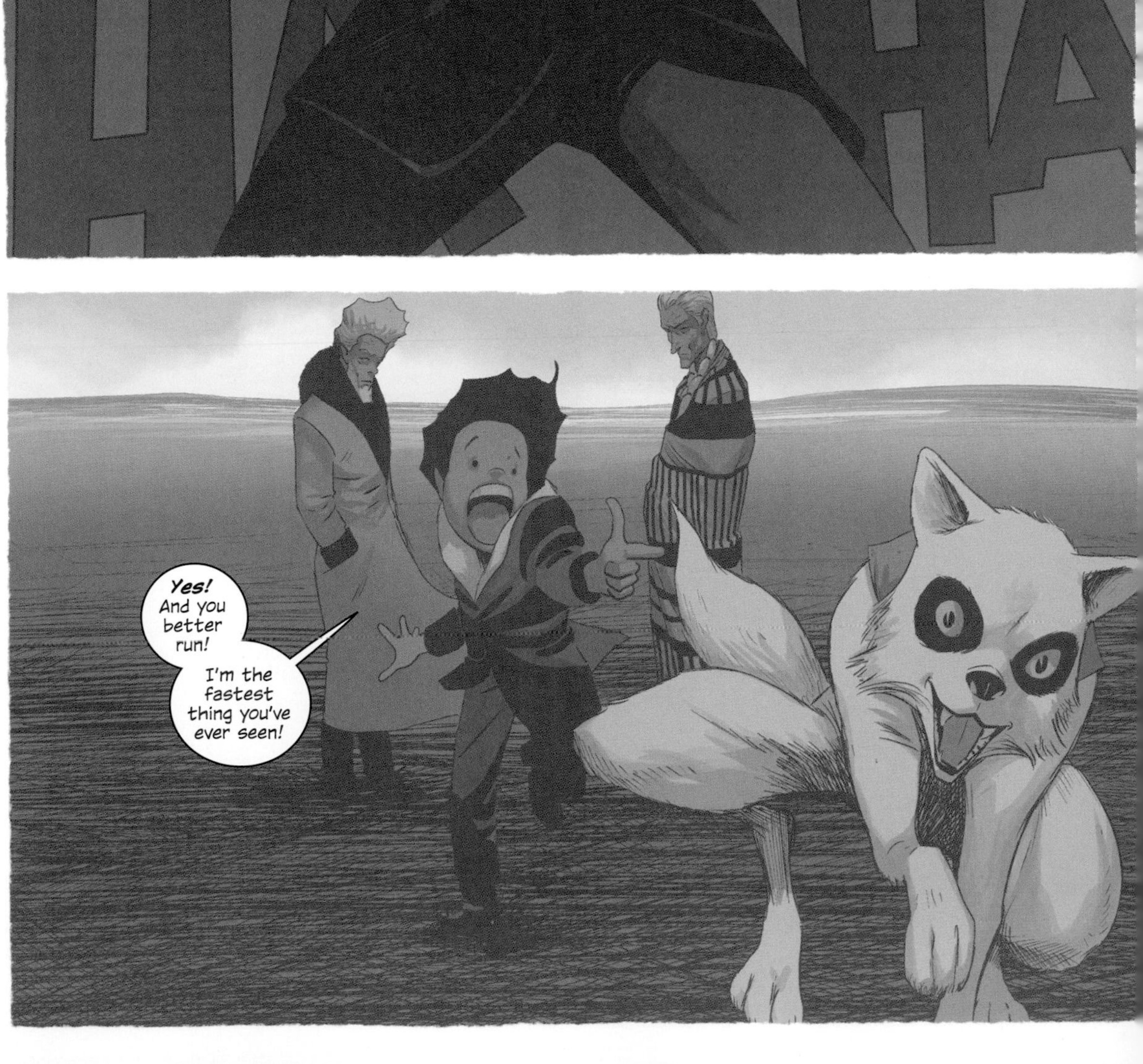
Yes! And you better run!
I'm the fastest thing you've ever seen!

I DON'T **BELIEVE** IN
THIS **ANYMORE**...

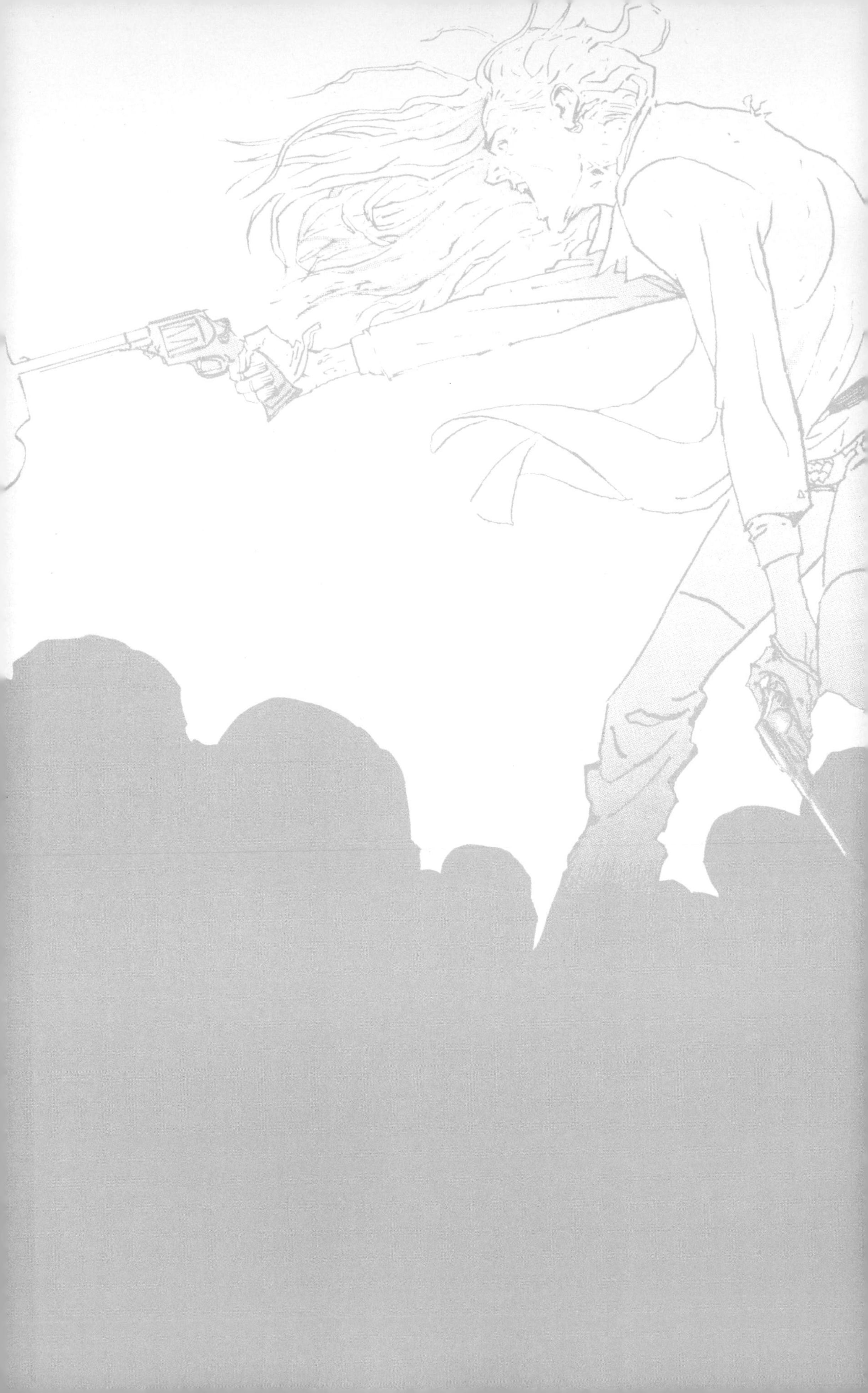

41

FORTY-ONE:
TO THE **VICTOR**,
GOES **EVERYTHING**

...BUT I DO **BELIEVE**
IN **YOU.**

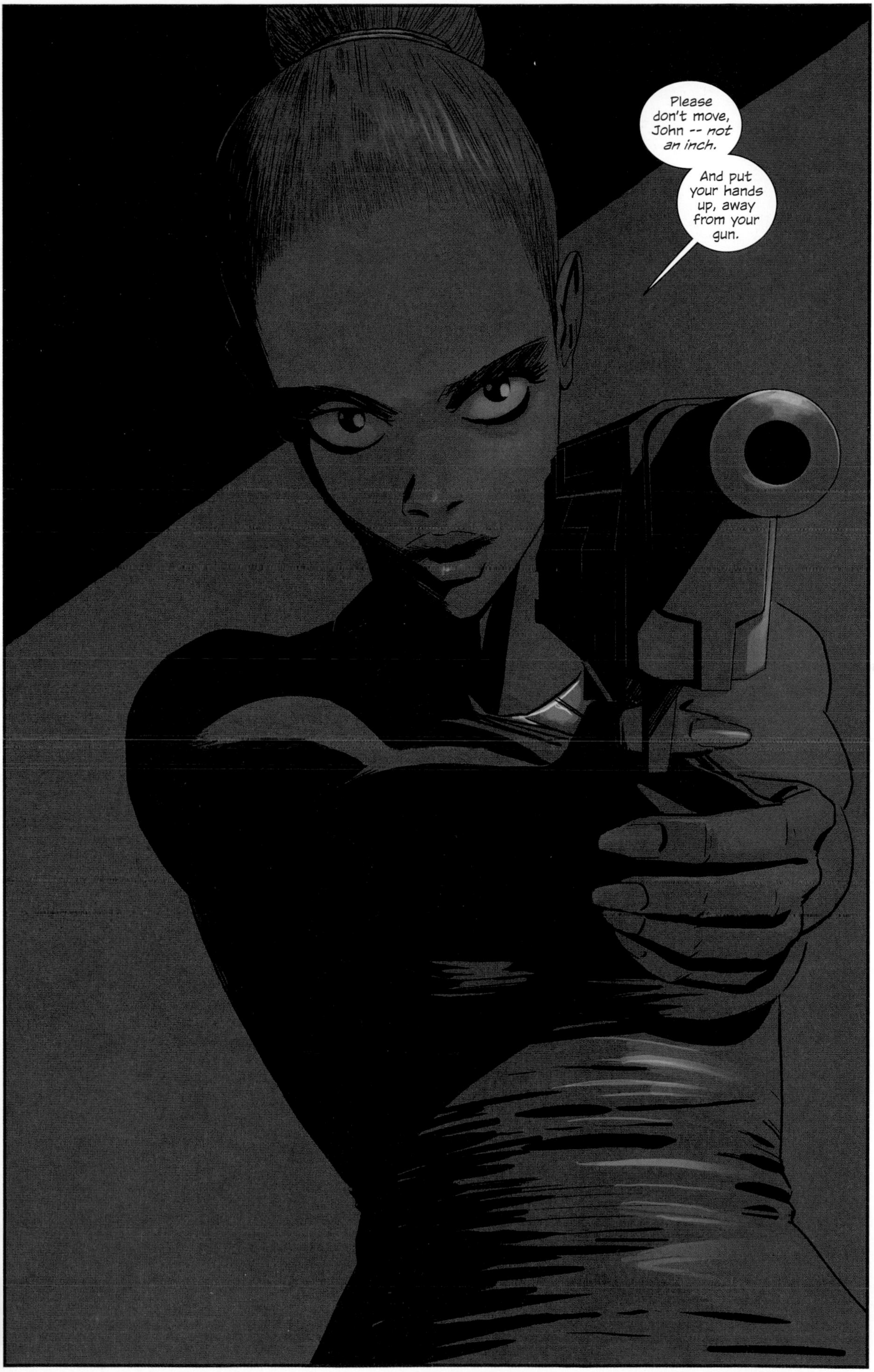
Please don't move, John -- *not an inch.*
And put your hands up, away from your gun.

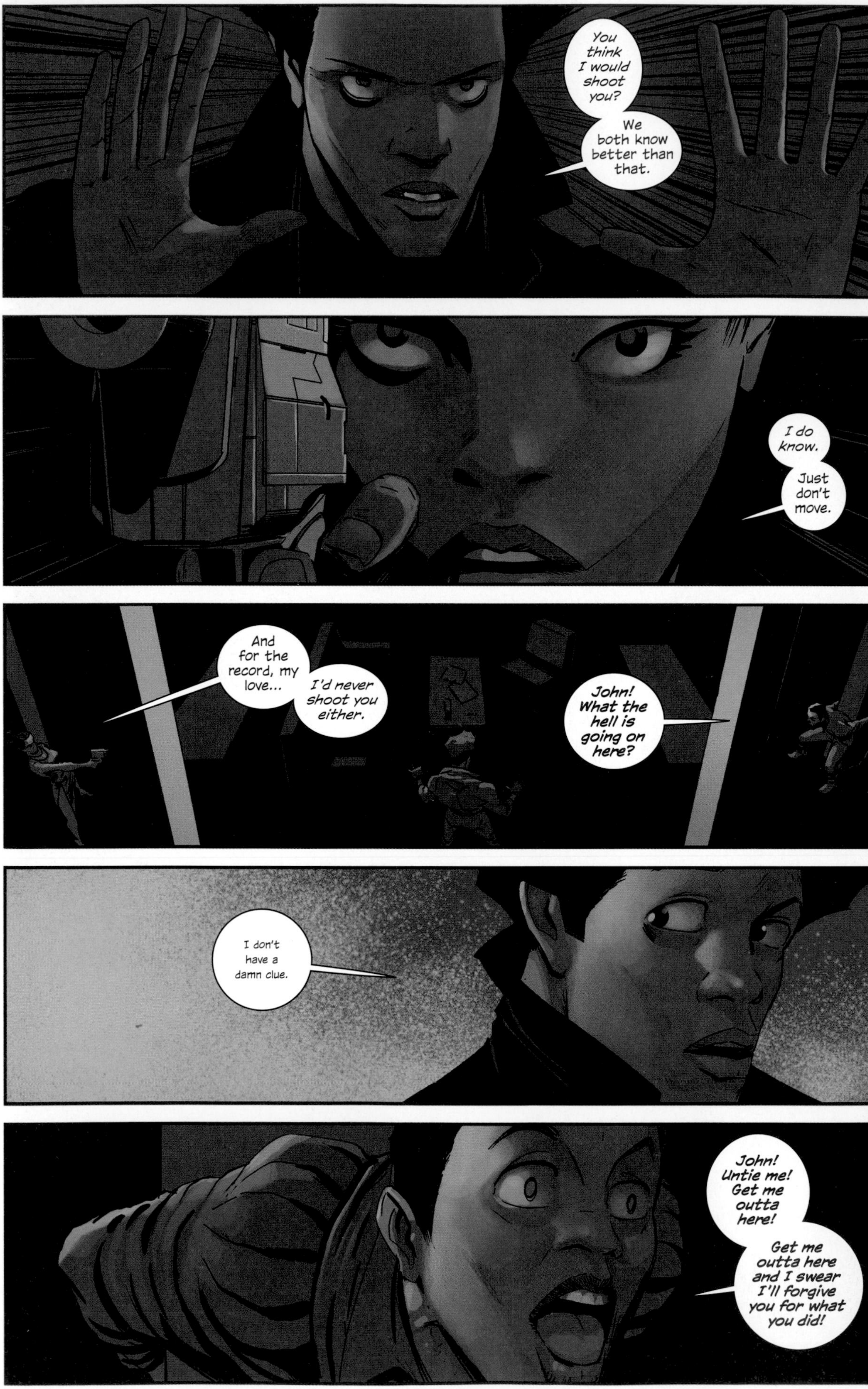

You think I would shoot you?
We both know better than that.
I do know.
Just don't move.
And for the record, my love...
I'd never shoot you either.
John! What the hell is going on here?
I don't have a damn clue.
John! Untie me! Get me outta here!
Get me outta here and I swear I'll forgive you for what you did!

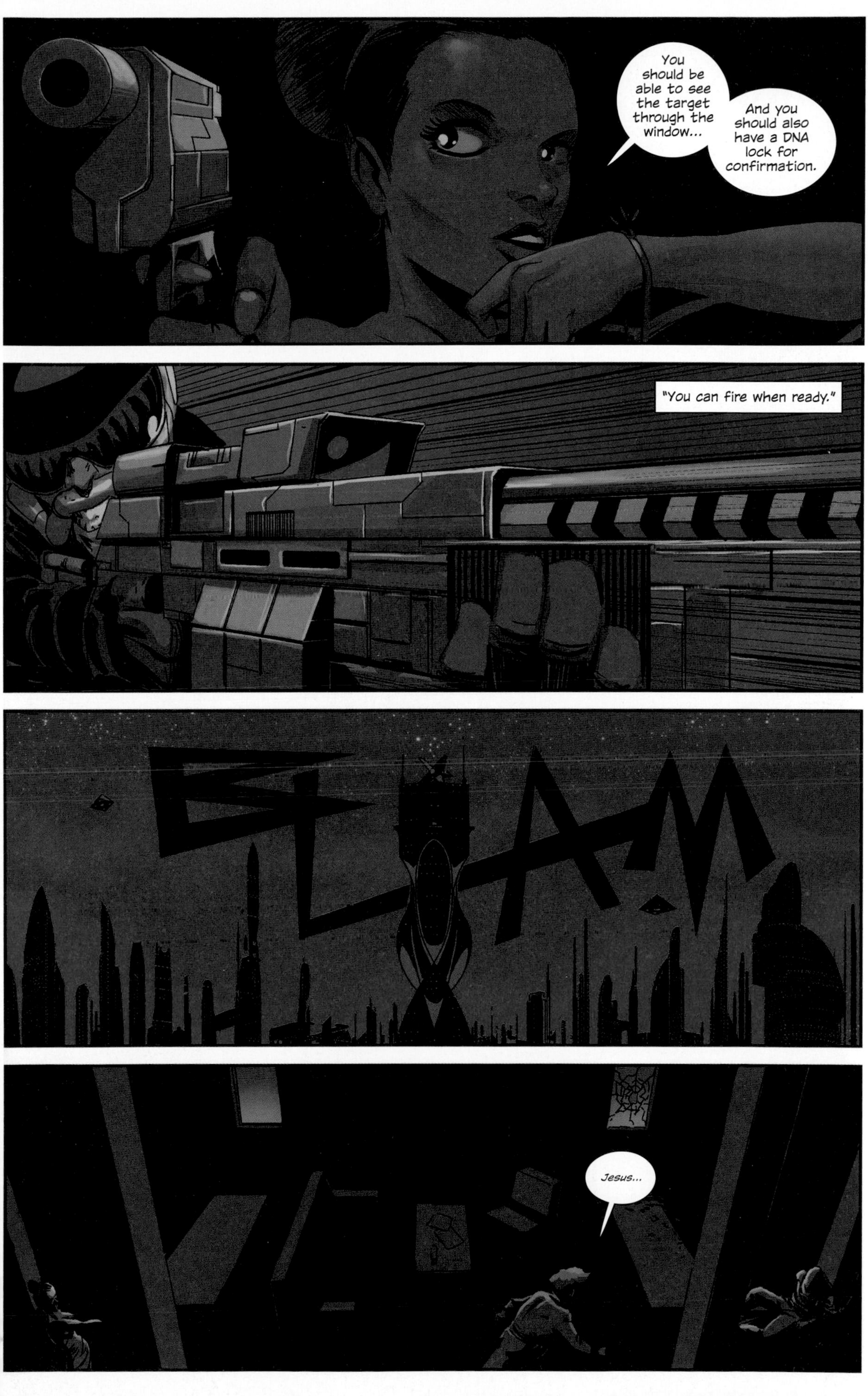
You should be able to see the target through the window...
And you should also have a DNA lock for confirmation.
"You can fire when ready."
BLAM
Jesus...

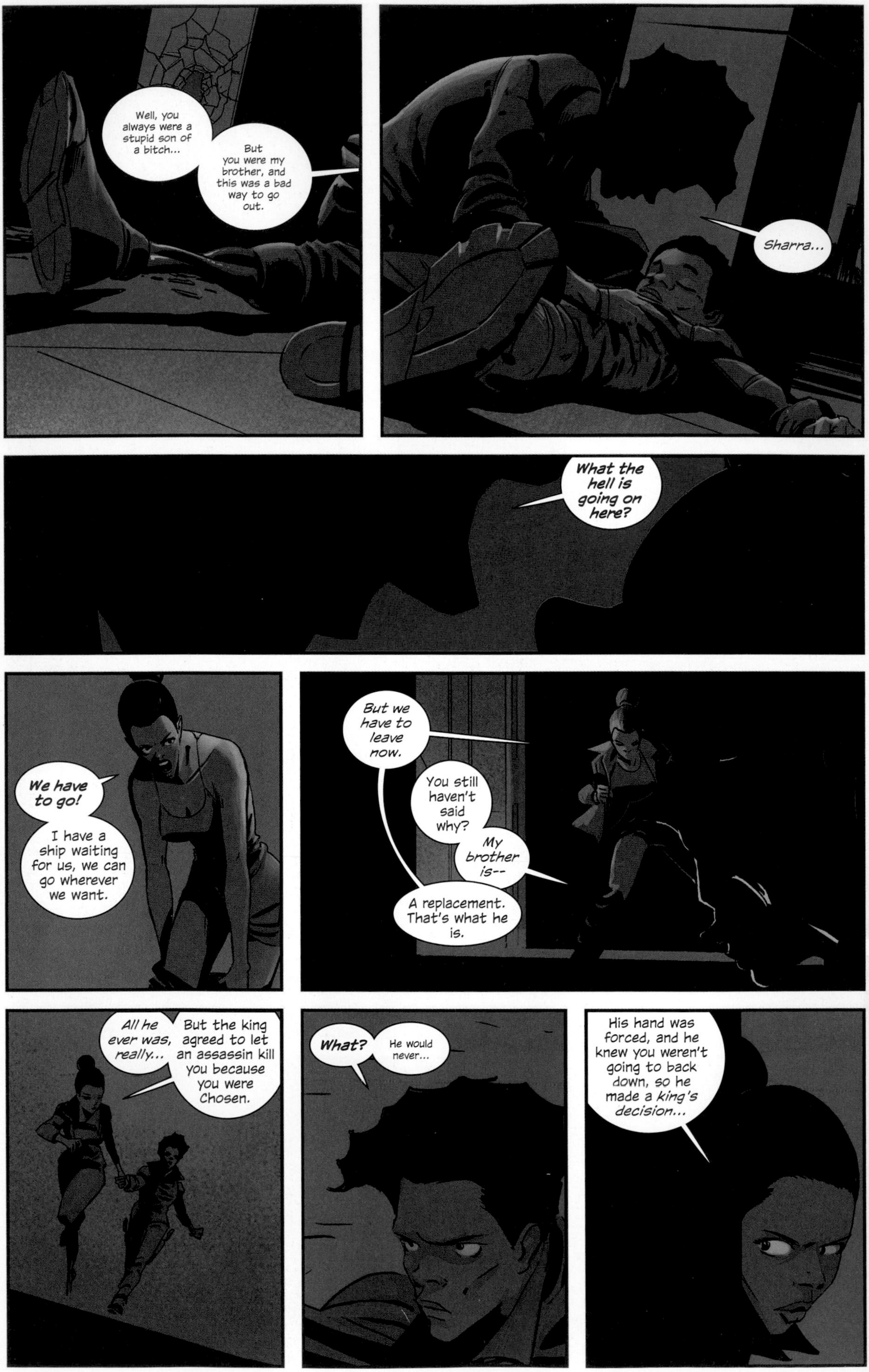
Well, you always were a stupid son of a bitch...
But you were my brother, and this was a bad way to go out.
Sharra...
What the hell is going on here?
We have to go!
I have a ship waiting for us, we can go wherever we want.
But we have to leave now.
You still haven't said why?
My brother is--
A replacement. That's what he is.
All he ever was, really...
But the king agreed to let an assassin kill you because you were Chosen.
What?
He would never...
His hand was forced, and he knew you weren't going to back down, so he made a king's decision...

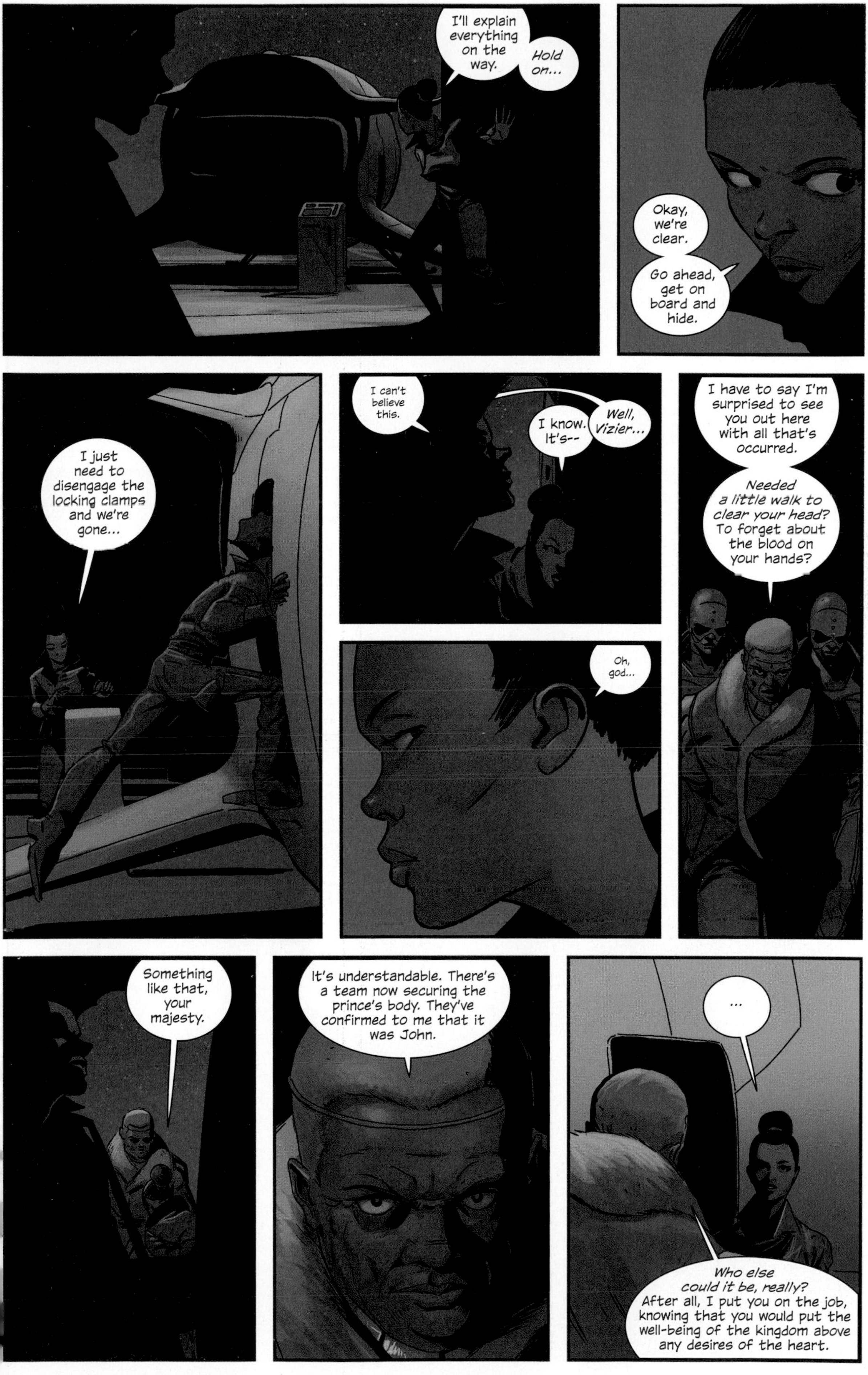
I'll explain everything on the way.
Hold on...
Okay, we're clear.
Go ahead, get on board and hide.
I just need to disengage the locking clamps and we're gone...
I can't believe this.
I know. It's--
Well, Vizier...
I have to say I'm surprised to see you out here with all that's occurred.
Needed a little walk to clear your head? To forget about the blood on your hands?
Oh, god...
Something like that, your majesty.
It's understandable. There's a team now securing the prince's body. They've confirmed to me that it was John.
...
Who else could it be, really? After all, I put you on the job, knowing that you would put the well-being of the kingdom above any desires of the heart.

Still... I will miss the boy. He would have, one day, made a formidable king.

And while I don't believe in miracles, if by one he was to appear someday, healthy and whole...

I do believe, in spite of the hard words he had for me the last time we spoke, I would embrace him and welcome him home to reclaim his rightful seat.

If only, my king.

Yes. If only...

Well, I have much ugly work to do this evening, but you take the night and mourn. However, there is one thing I do want you to remember...

Viziers clean up messes, they do not make them.

I understand, your majesty.

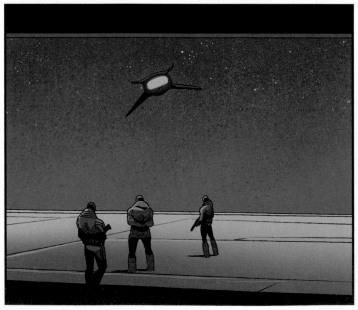

Good girl.

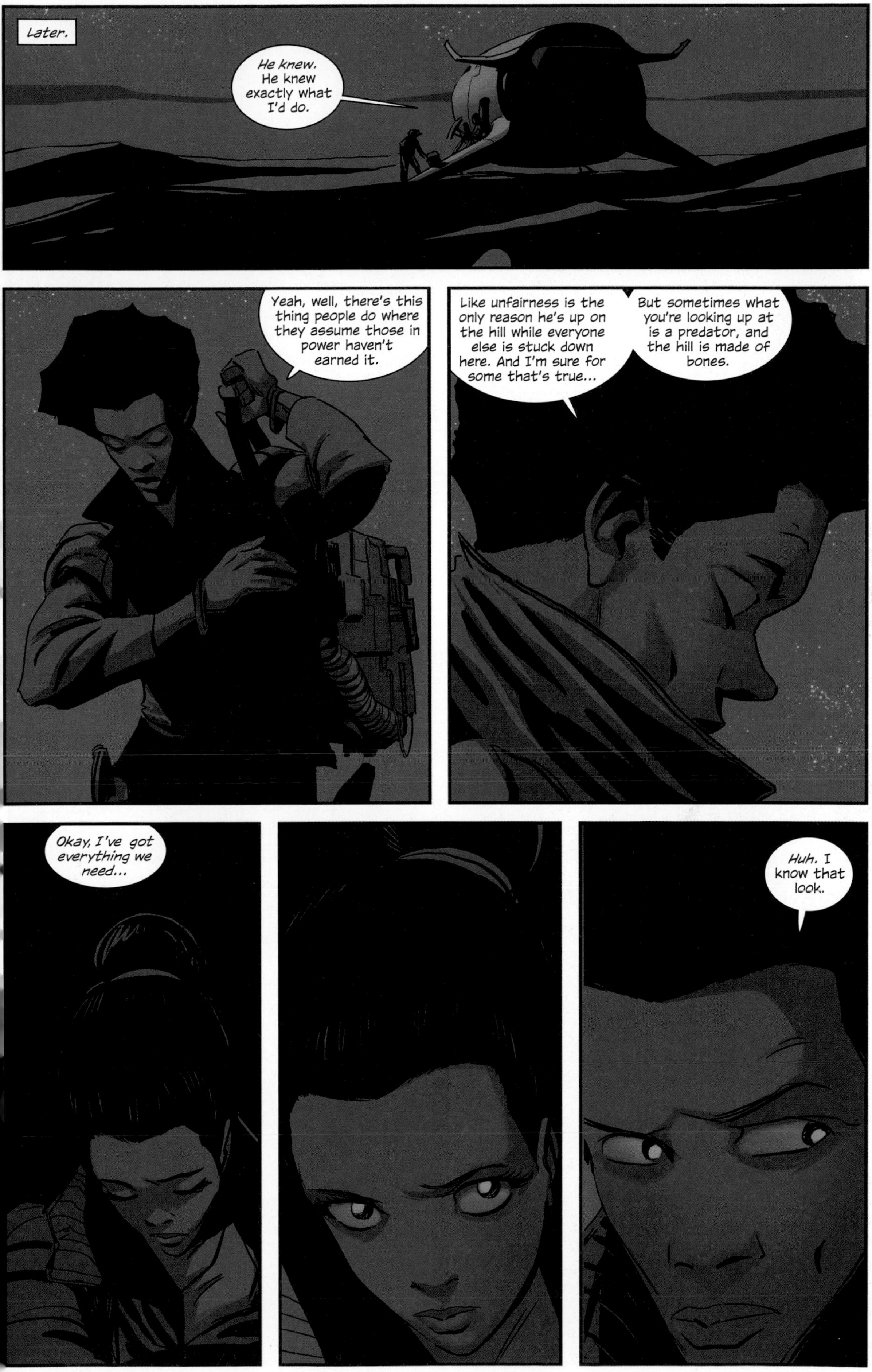
Later.
He knew. He knew exactly what I'd do.
Yeah, well, there's this thing people do where they assume those in power haven't earned it.
Like unfairness is the only reason he's up on the hill while everyone else is stuck down here. And I'm sure for some that's true...
But sometimes what you're looking up at is a predator, and the hill is made of bones.
Okay, I've got everything we need...
Huh. I know that look.

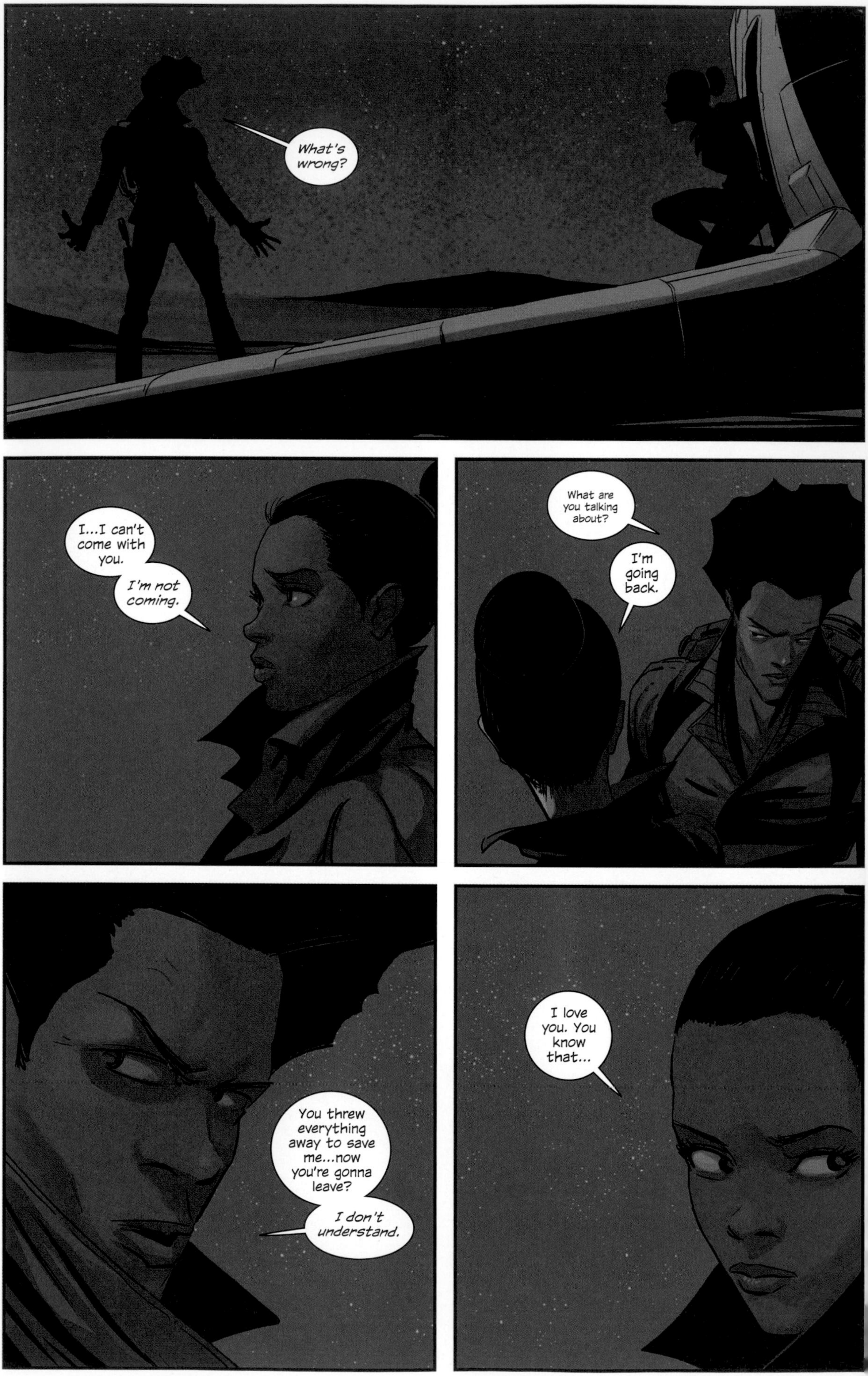

What's wrong?
I...I can't come with you.
I'm not coming.
What are you talking about?
I'm going back.
You threw everything away to save me...now you're gonna leave?
I don't understand.
I love you. You know that...

But what I am -- who I am -- is in the Kingdom, just like I know what you are is *out* here.

I risked everything to save you -- *I had to do that* -- but I can't give up what I am.

All I can do is free you...

And so now you're free.

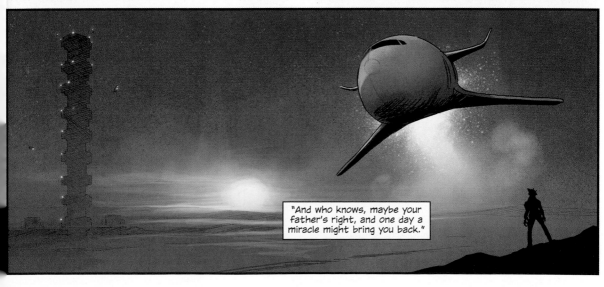

"And who knows, maybe your father's right, and one day a miracle might bring you back."

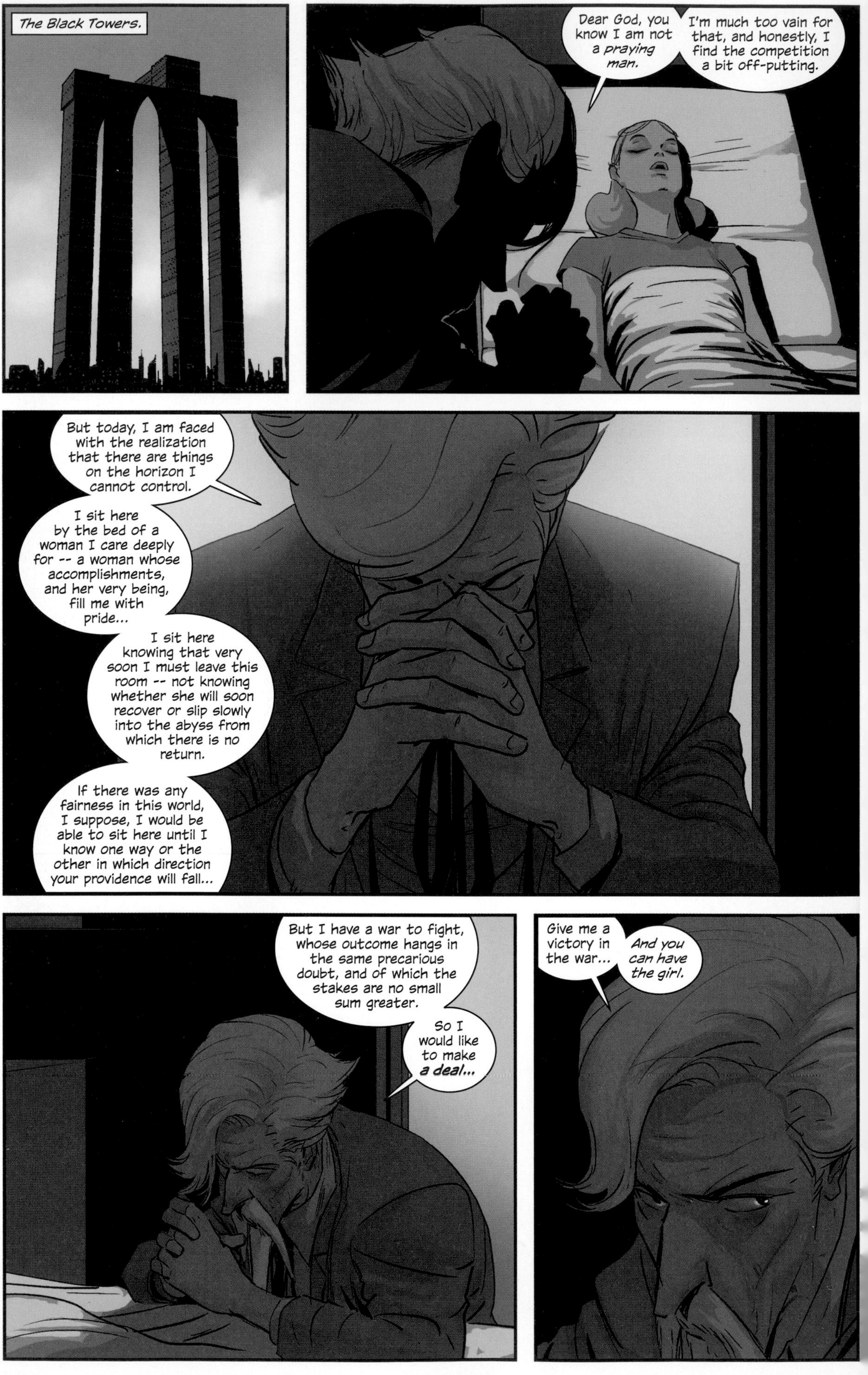
The Black Towers.
Dear God, you know I am not a *praying* man.
I'm much too vain for that, and honestly, I find the competition a bit off-putting.
But today, I am faced with the realization that there are things on the horizon I cannot control.
I sit here by the bed of a woman I care deeply for -- a woman whose accomplishments, and her very being, fill me with pride...
I sit here knowing that very soon I must leave this room -- not knowing whether she will soon recover or slip slowly into the abyss from which there is no return.
If there was any fairness in this world, I suppose, I would be able to sit here until I know one way or the other in which direction your providence will fall...
But I have a war to fight, whose outcome hangs in the same precarious doubt, and of which the stakes are no small sum greater.
So I would like to make **a deal...**
Give me a victory in the war...
And you can have the girl.

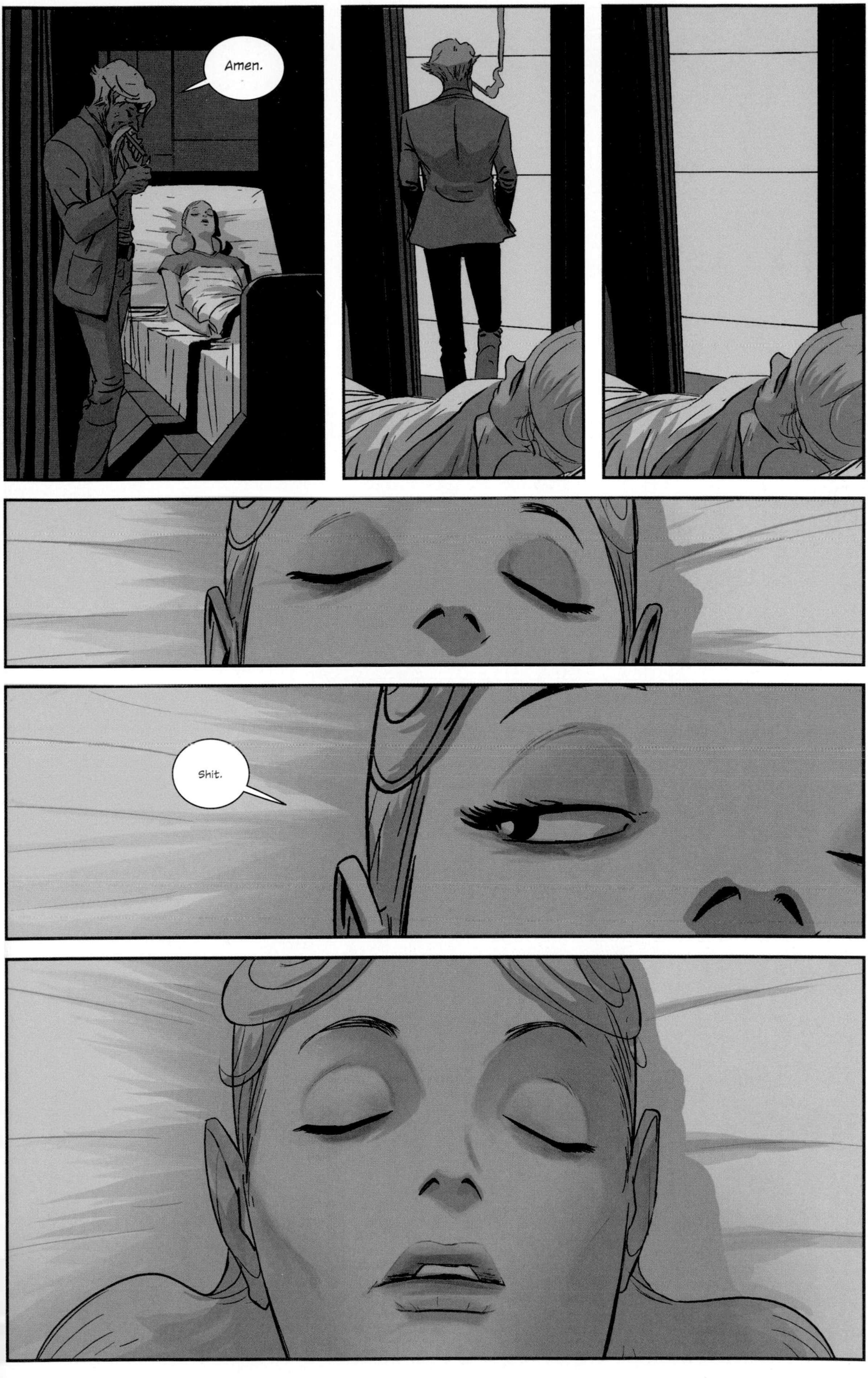
Amen.
Shit.

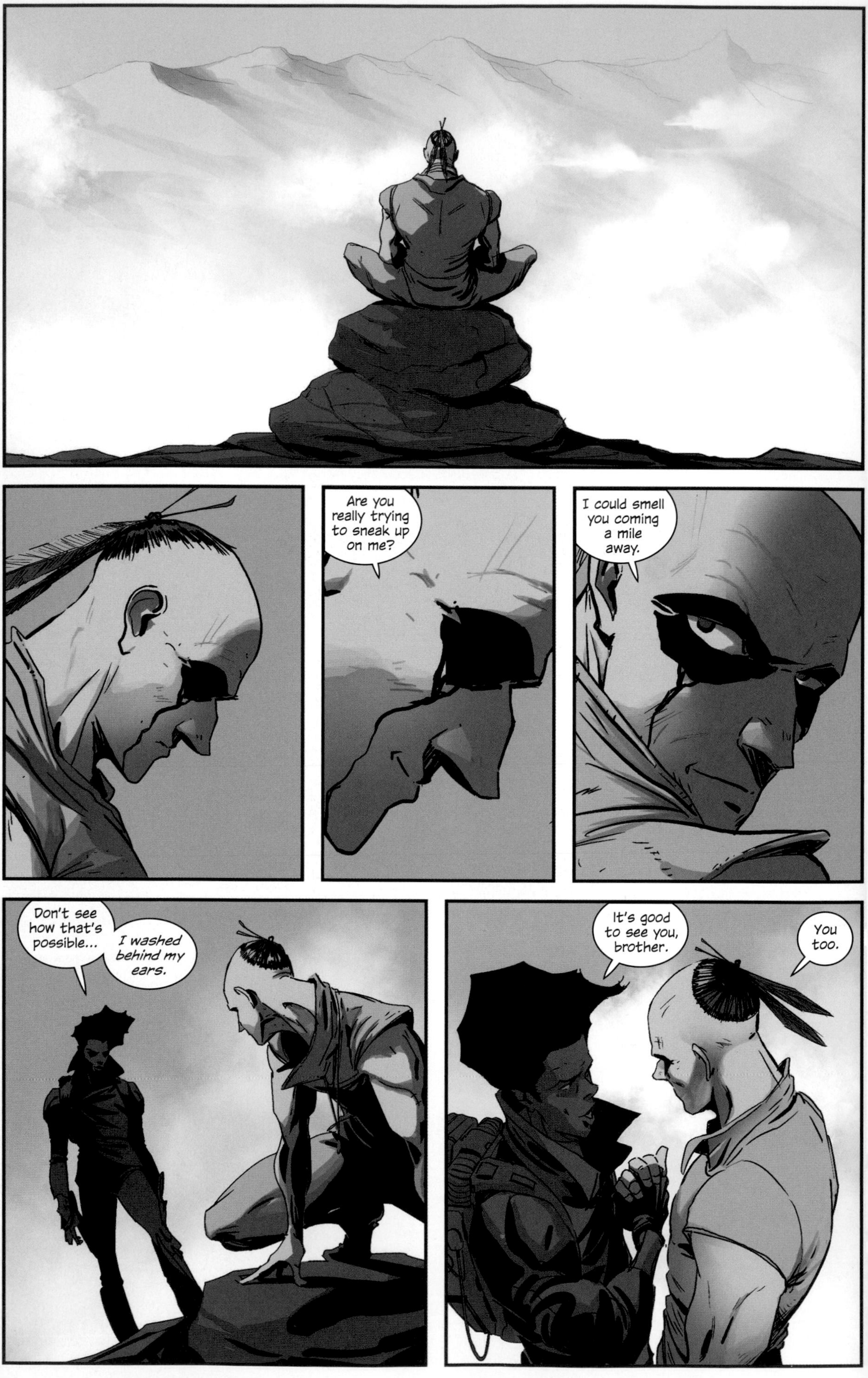
Are you really trying to sneak up on me?
I could smell you coming a mile away.
Don't see how that's possible...
I washed behind my ears.
It's good to see you, brother.
You too.

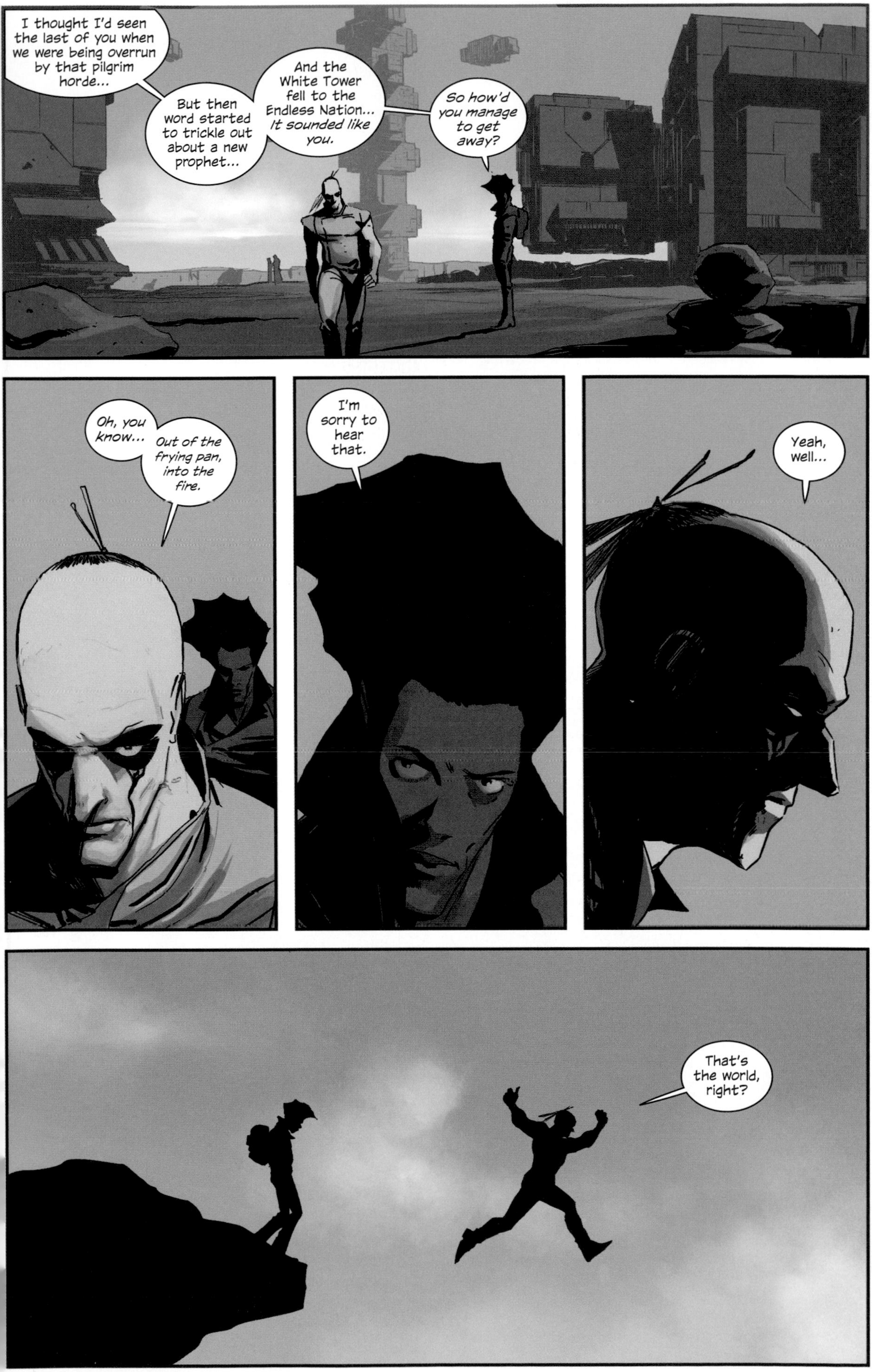
I thought I'd seen the last of you when we were being overrun by that pilgrim horde...
But then word started to trickle out about a new prophet...
And the White Tower fell to the Endless Nation... It sounded like you.
So how'd you manage to get away?
Oh, you know...
Out of the frying pan, into the fire.
I'm sorry to hear that.
Yeah, well...
That's the world, right?

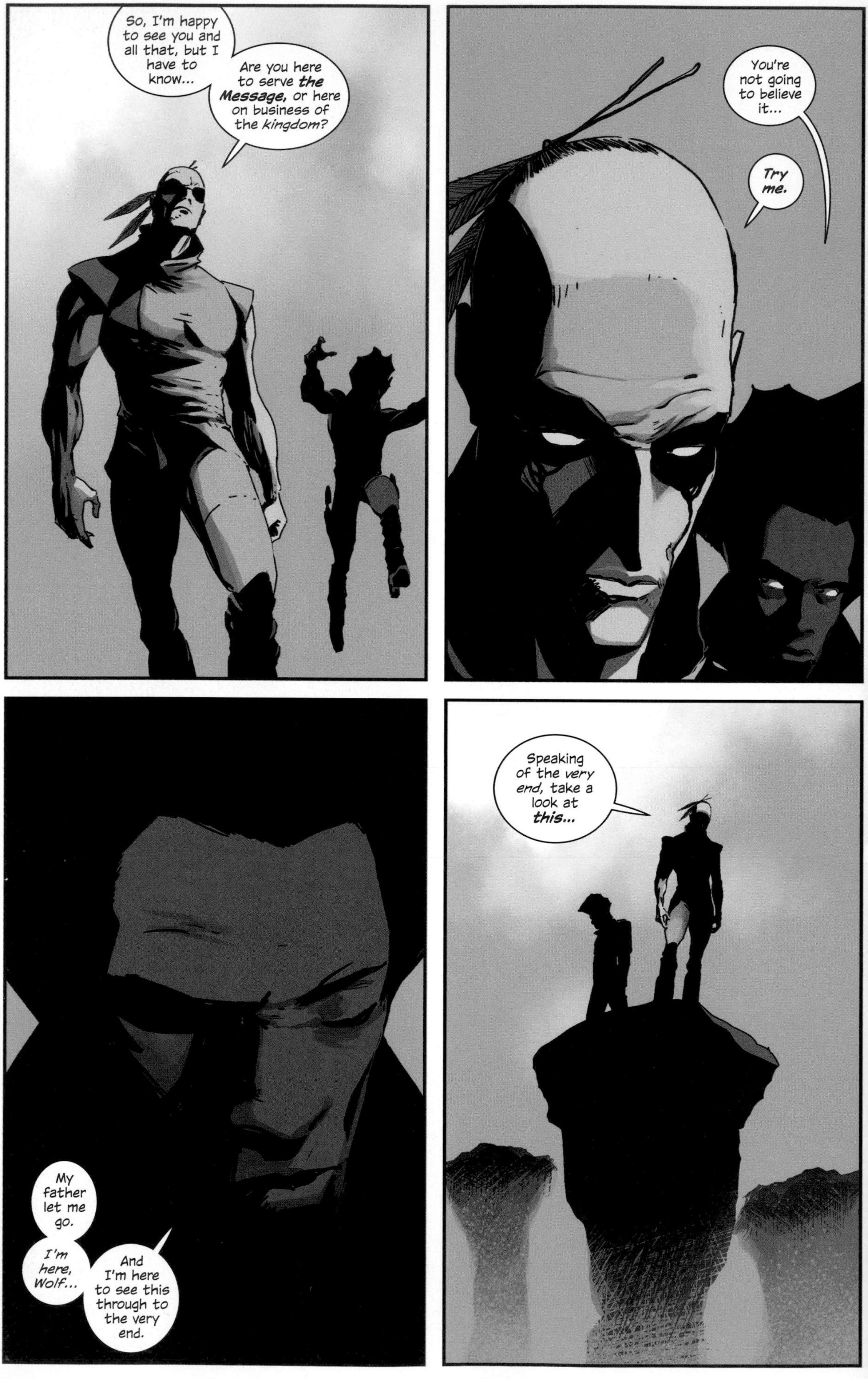

So, I'm happy to see you and all that, but I have to know...
Are you here to serve **the Message,** or here on business of the *kingdom?*
You're not going to believe it...
Try me.
My father let me go.
I'm here, Wolf...
And I'm here to see this through to the very end.
Speaking of the *very end*, take a look at ***this...***

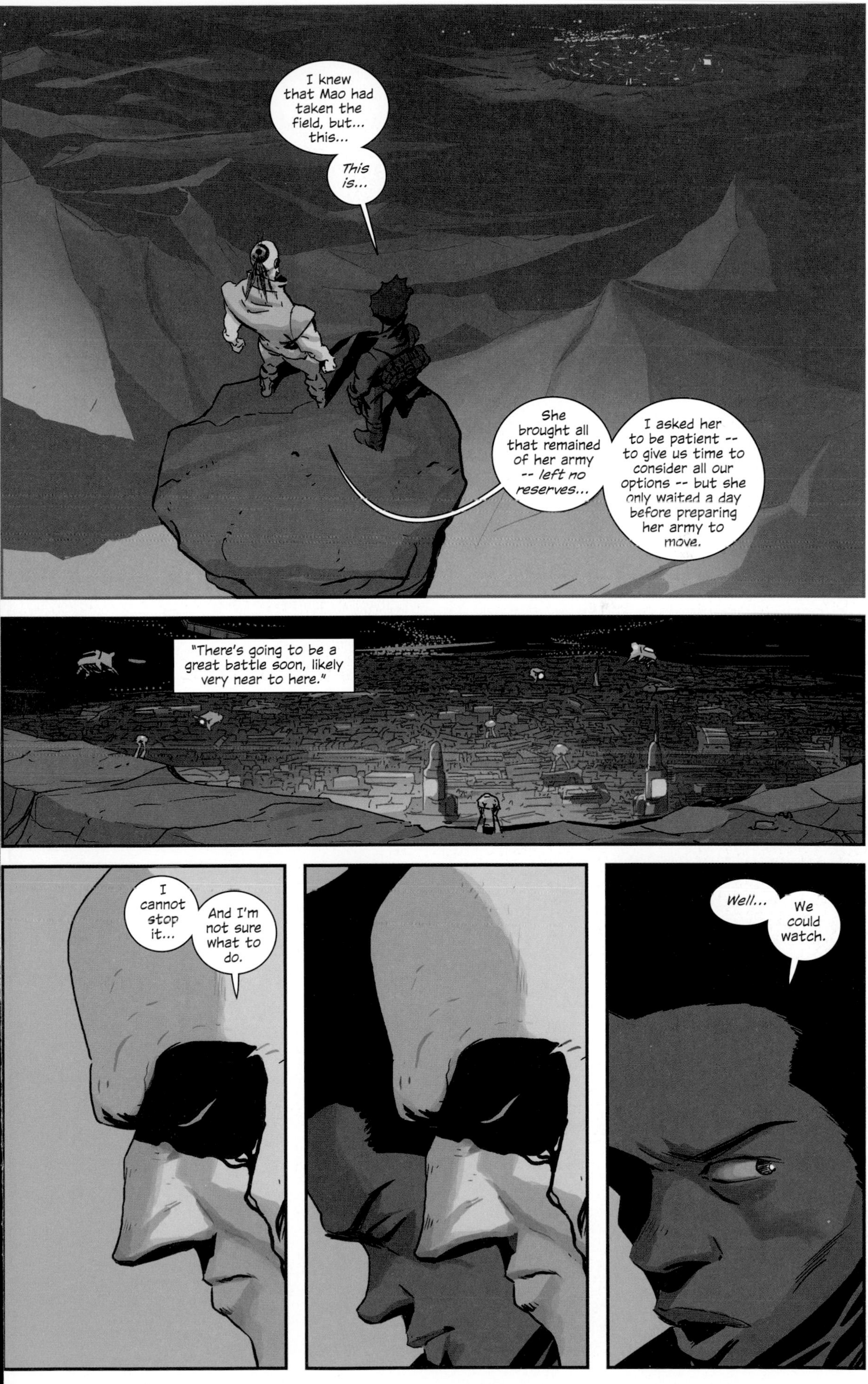
I knew that Mao had taken the field, but... this...
This is...
She brought all that remained of her army -- left no reserves...
I asked her to be patient -- to give us time to consider all our options -- but she only waited a day before preparing her army to move.
"There's going to be a great battle soon, likely very near to here."
I cannot stop it...
And I'm not sure what to do.
Well...
We could watch.

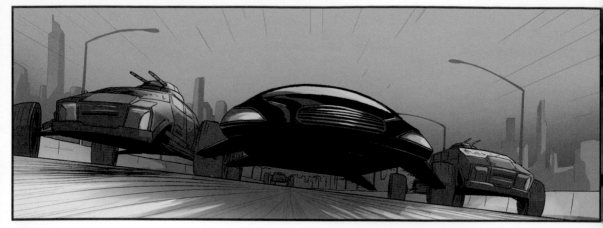

I have to say, I'm feeling something I haven't felt in years.

I suppose that's a byproduct of a long winter -- one of those instances of having not used a certain muscle for quite some time.

I've spent decades planning, and for what? *Moments like these* -- where the old gunfighter gets to pull his piece one last time.

Some might call witnessing such a thing a *privilege.*

But I must say, you look ungrateful, old friend.

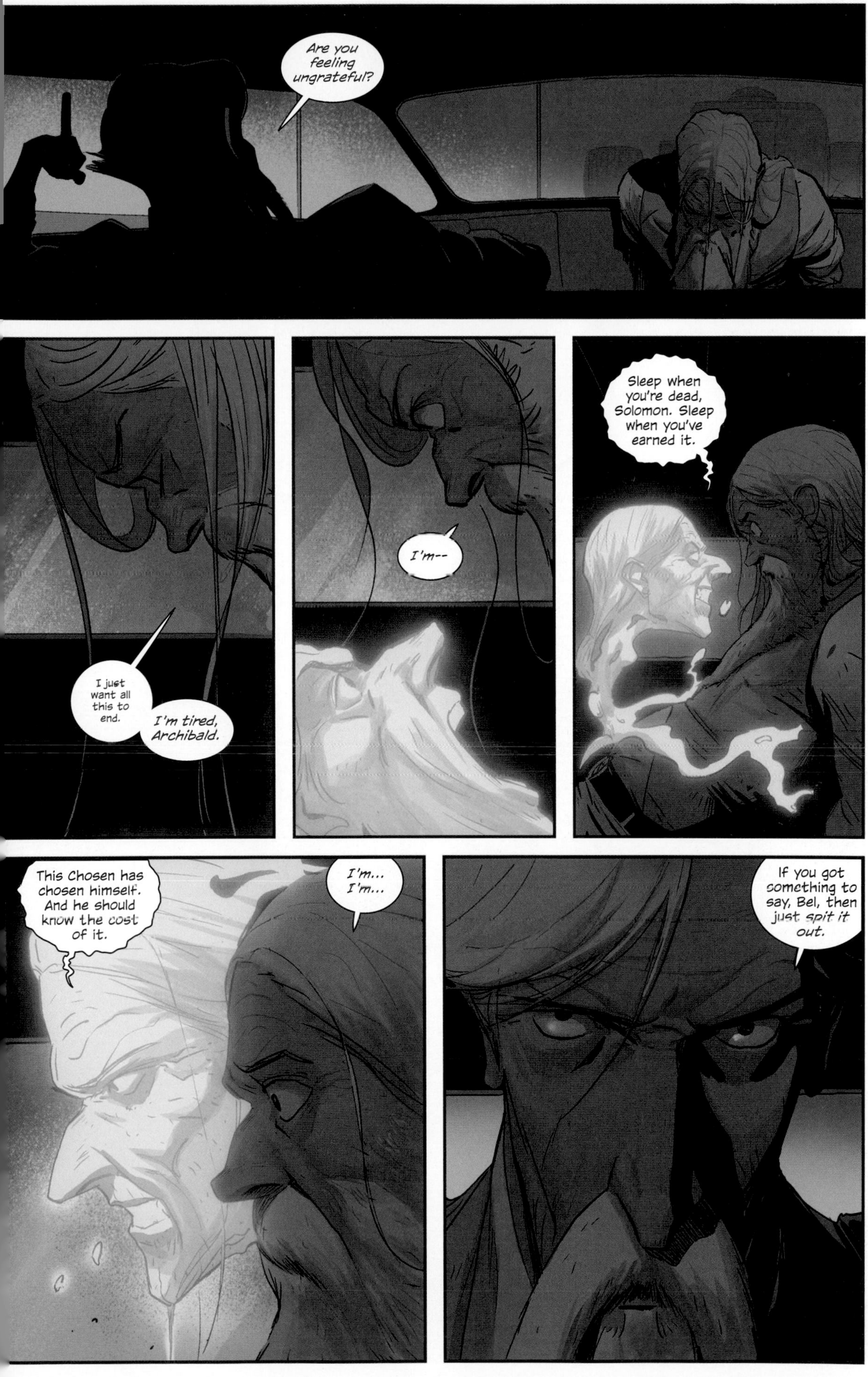
Are you feeling ungrateful?
I'm tired, Archibald.
I just want all this to end.
I'm--
Sleep when you're dead, Solomon. Sleep when you've earned it.
This Chosen has chosen himself. And he should know the cost of it.
I'm... I'm...
If you got something to say, Bel, then just spit it out.

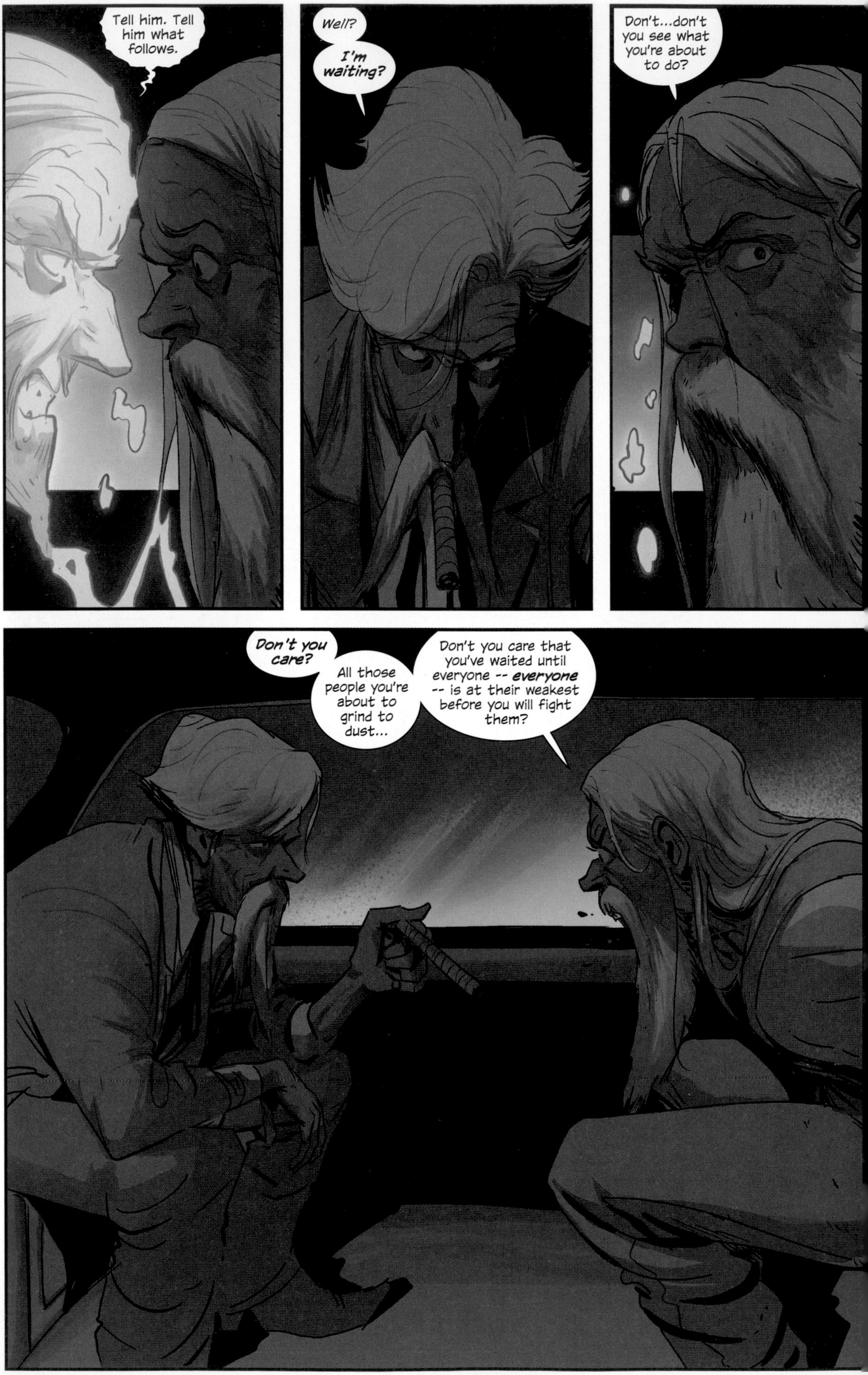
Tell him. Tell him what follows.
Well?
I'm waiting?
Don't...don't you see what you're about to do?
Don't you care?
All those people you're about to grind to dust...
Don't you care that you've waited until everyone -- everyone -- is at their weakest before you will fight them?

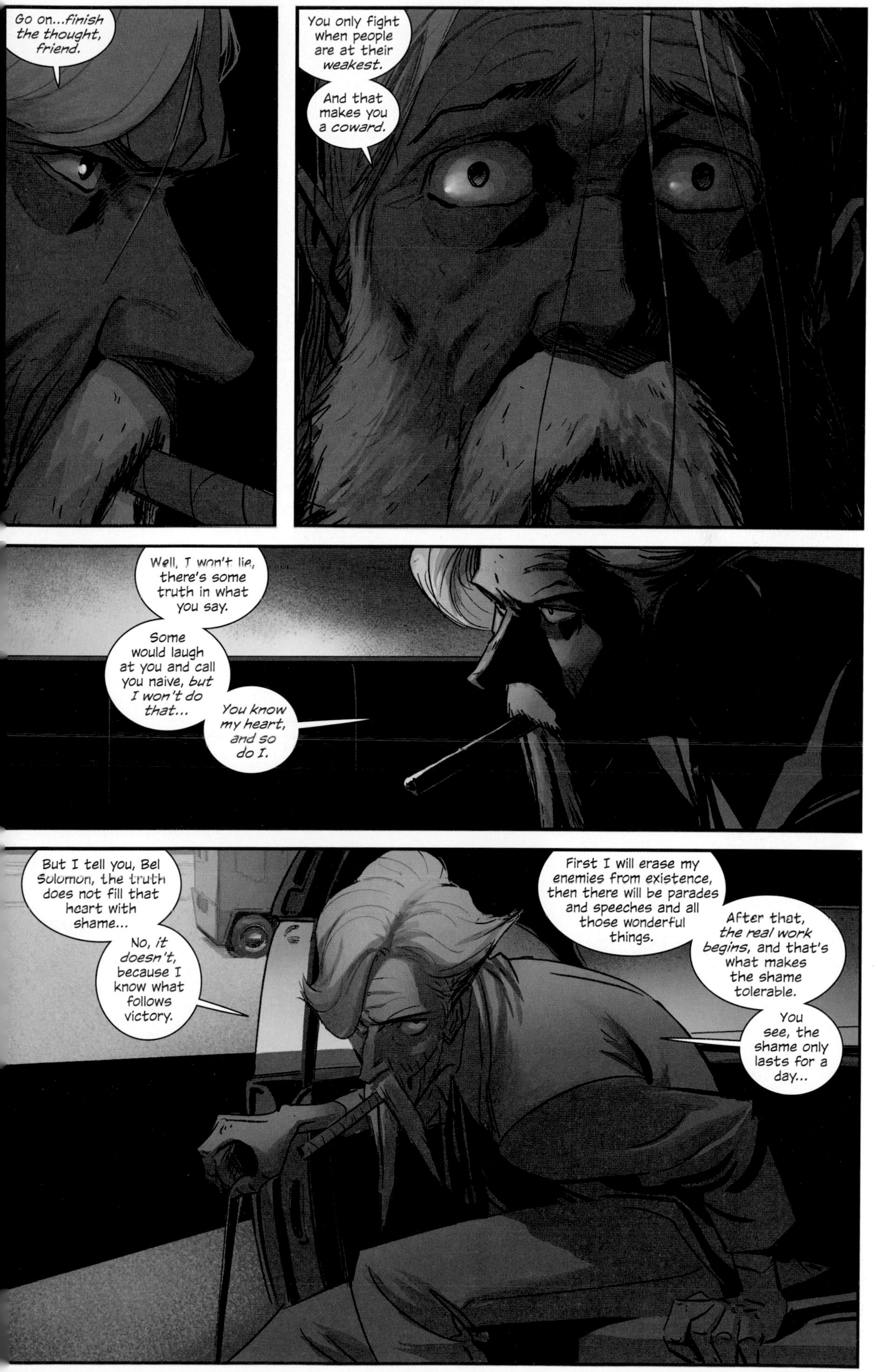
Go on...finish the thought, friend.
You only fight when people are at their weakest.
And that makes you a coward.
Well, I won't lie, there's some truth in what you say.
Some would laugh at you and call you naive, but I won't do that...
You know my heart, and so do I.
But I tell you, Bel Solomon, the truth does not fill that heart with shame...
No, it doesn't, because I know what follows victory.
First I will erase my enemies from existence, then there will be parades and speeches and all those wonderful things.
After that, the real work begins, and that's what makes the shame tolerable.
You see, the shame only lasts for a day...

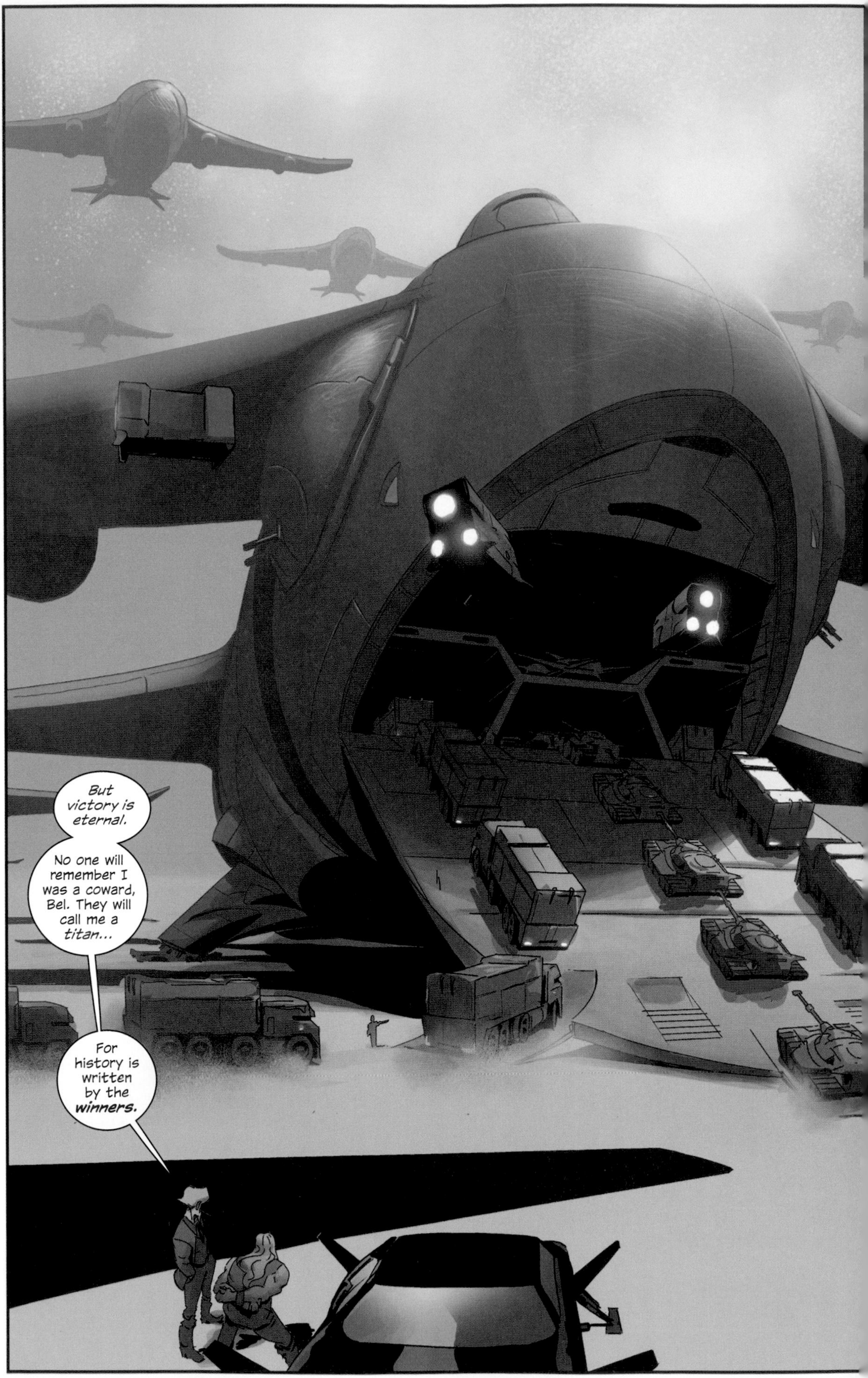
But victory is eternal.
No one will remember I was a coward, Bel. They will call me a titan...
For history is written by the winners.

THIS IS HOW IT **ENDS**,
WHERE IT ALL **BEGAN**.

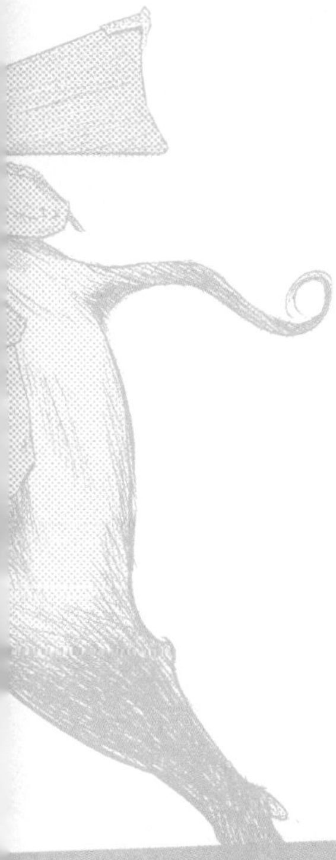

42

FORTY-TWO:
INTO THE **VALLEY**

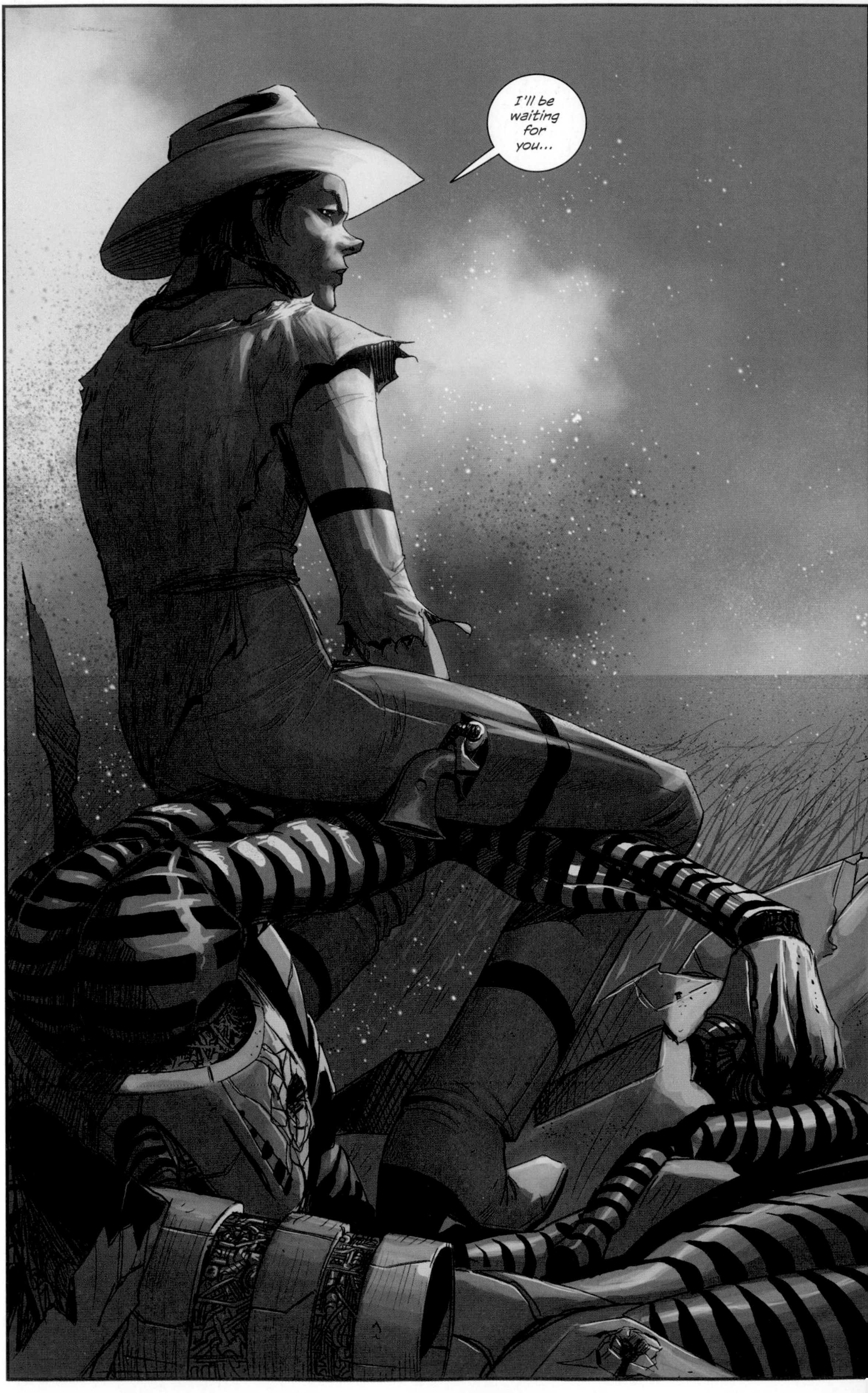
I'll be waiting for you...

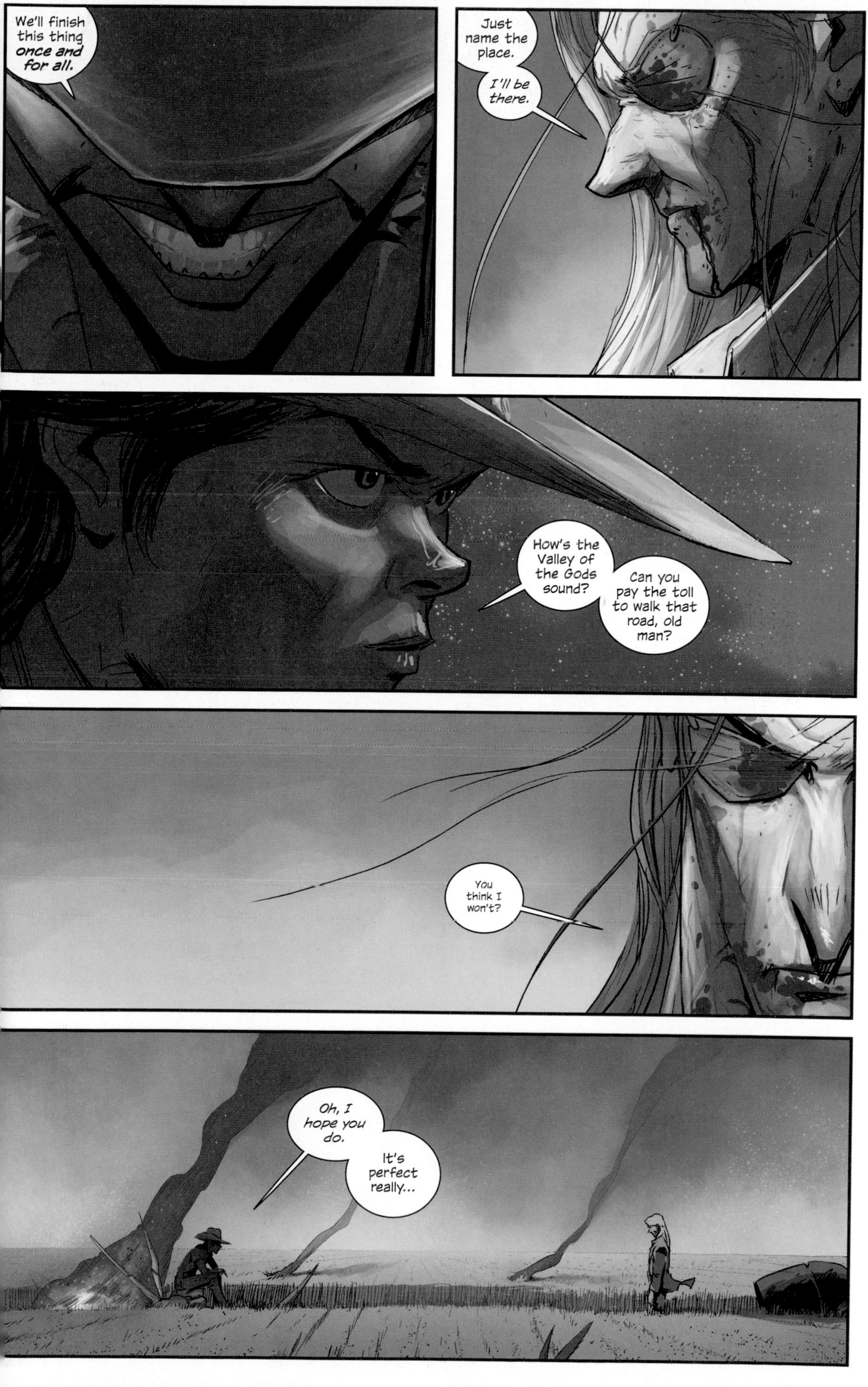
We'll finish this thing *once and for all.*
Just name the place.
I'll be there.
How's the Valley of the Gods sound?
Can you pay the toll to walk that road, old man?
You think I won't?
Oh, I hope you do.
It's perfect really...

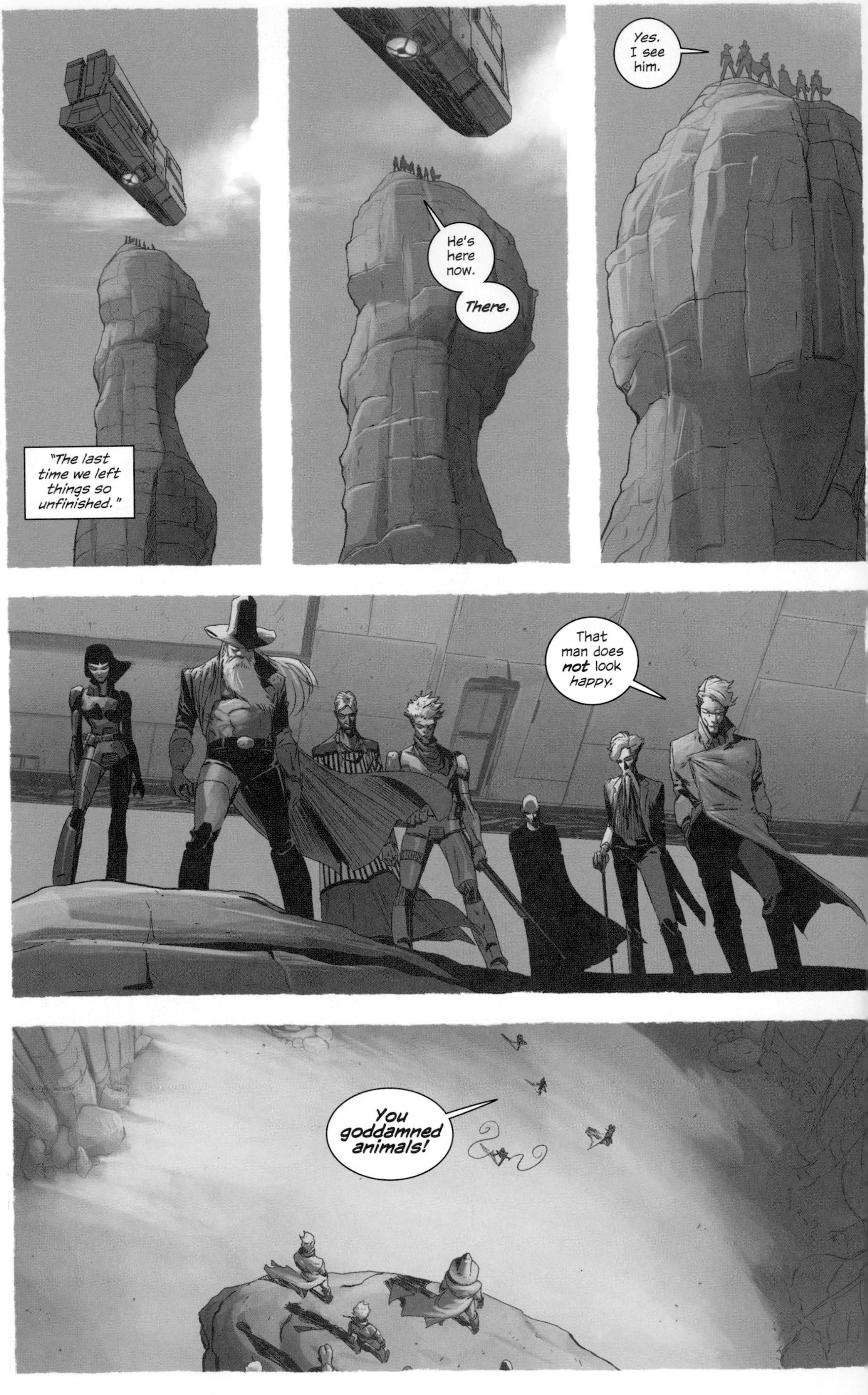
"The last time we left things so unfinished."
He's here now.
There.
Yes. I see him.
That man does **not** look happy.
You goddamned animals!

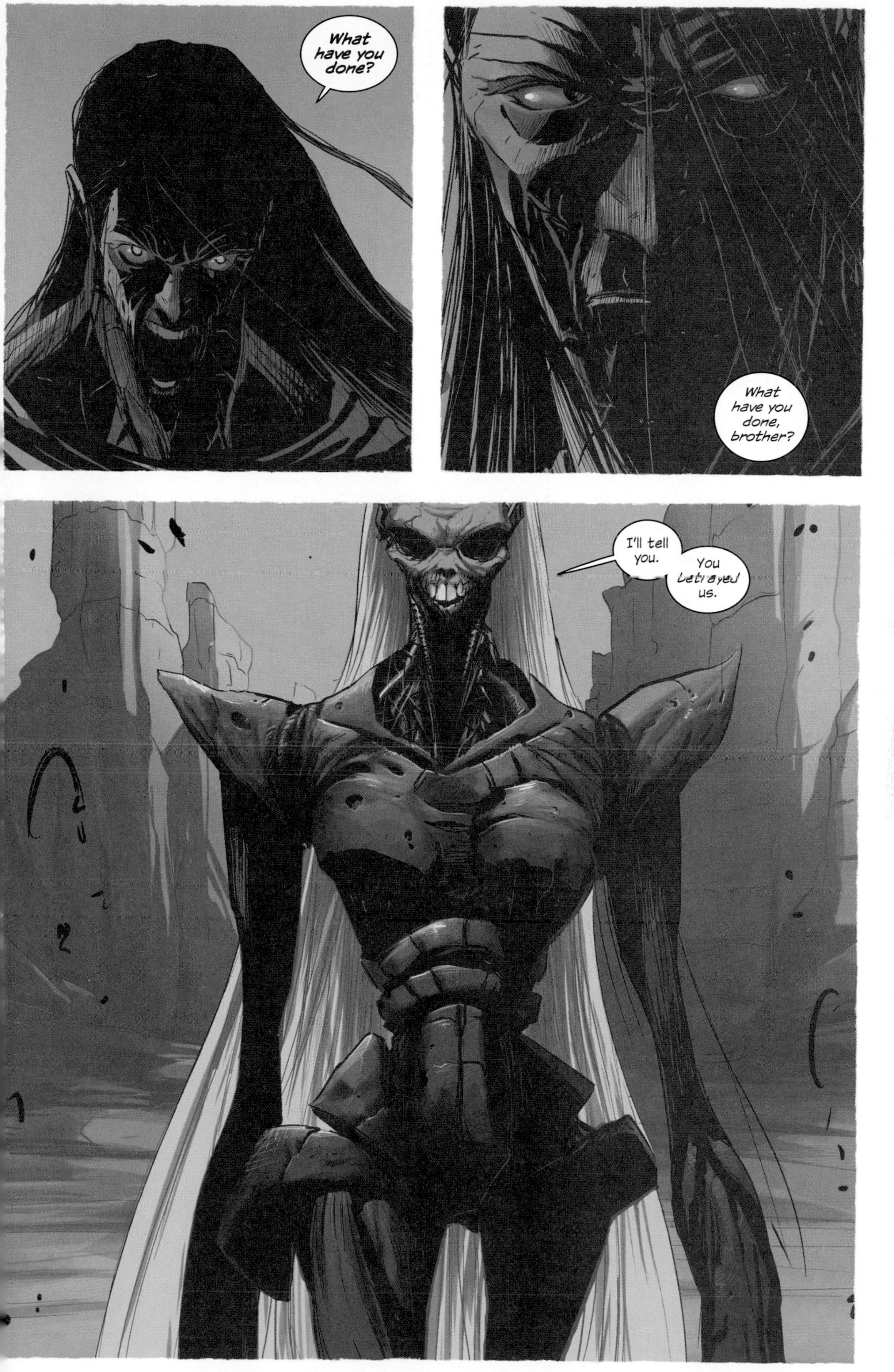
What have you done?
What have you done, brother?
I'll tell you.
You betrayed us.

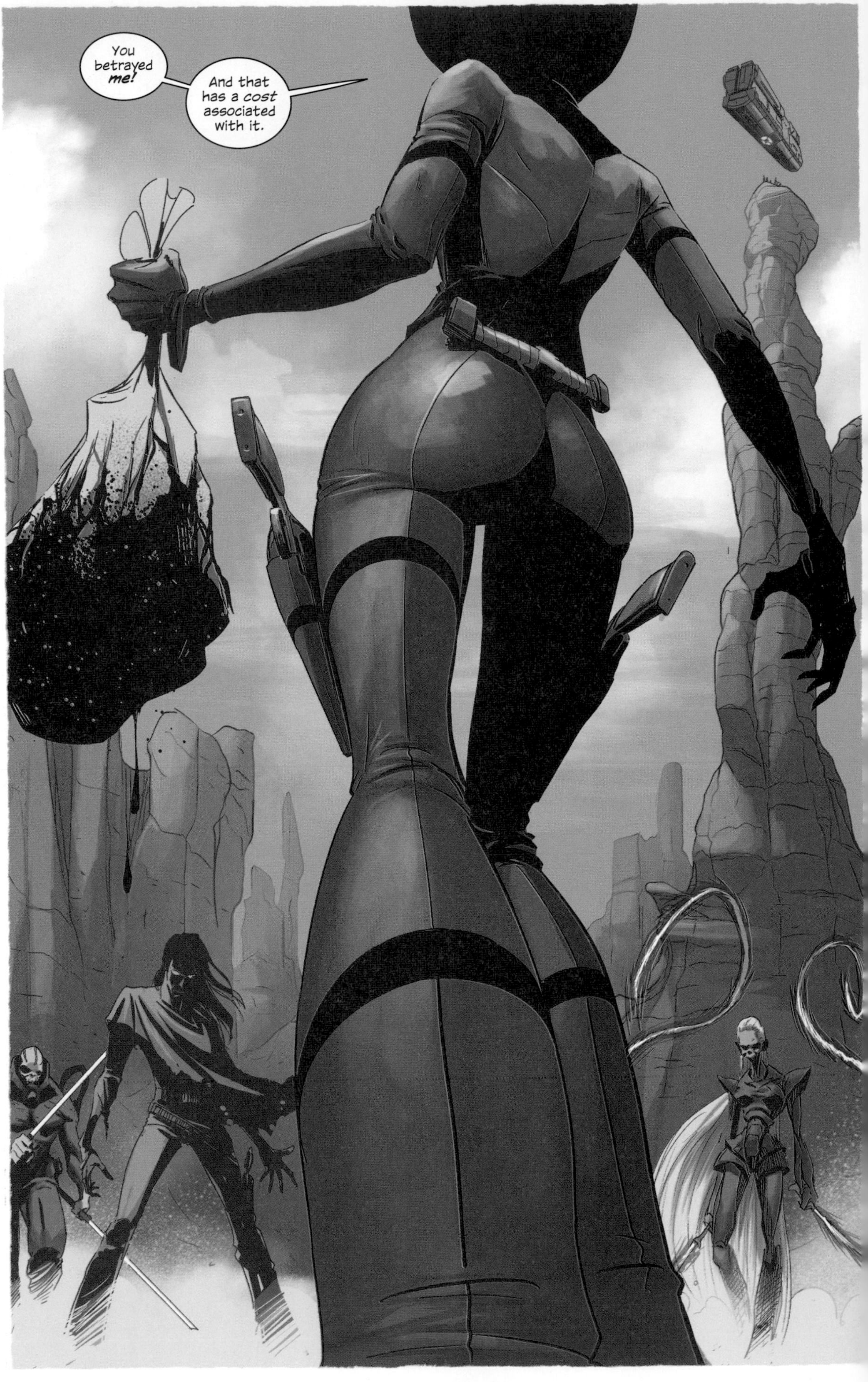
You betrayed *me!*
And that has a *cost* associated with it.

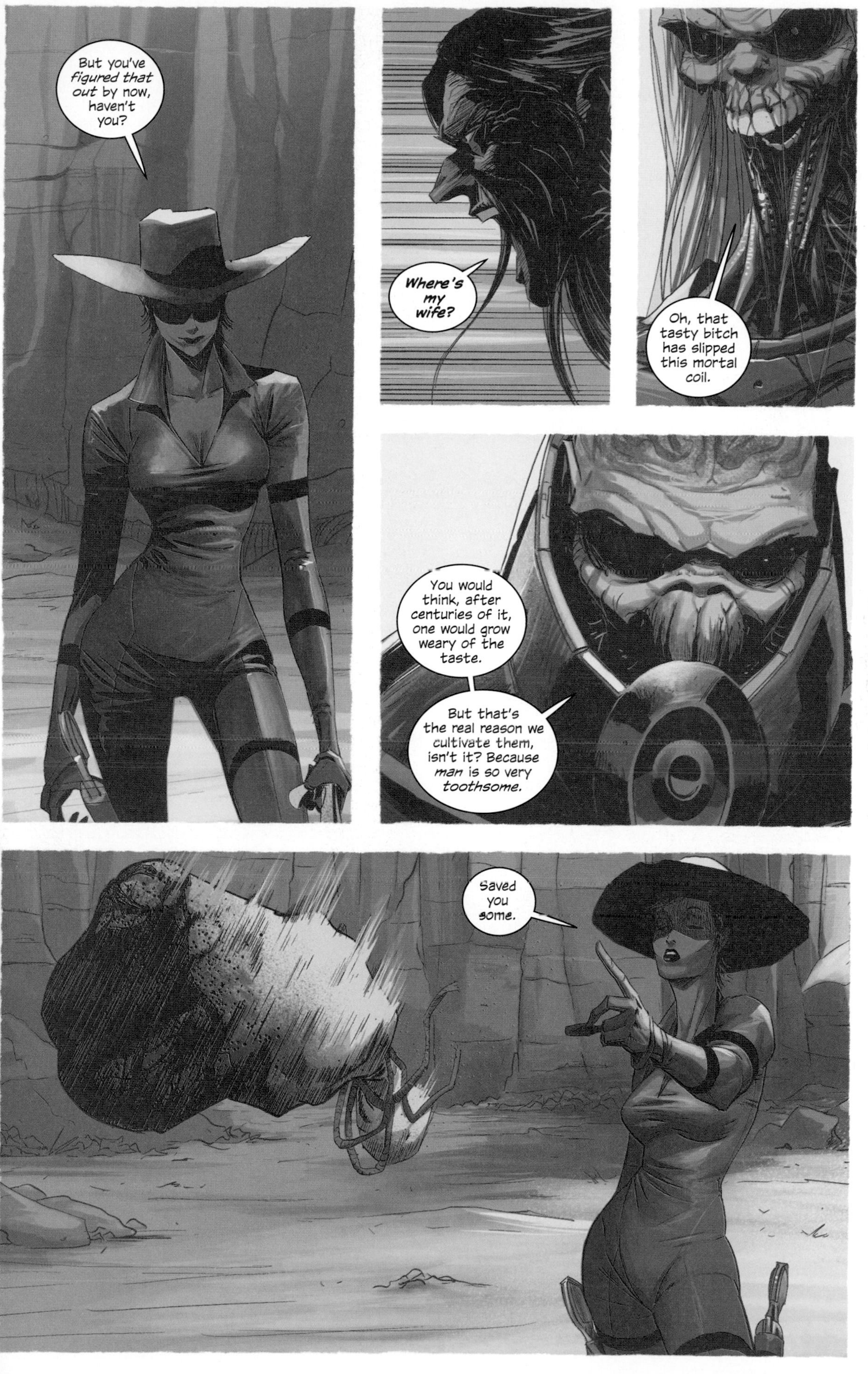
But you've *figured that out* by now, haven't you?
Where's my wife?
Oh, that tasty bitch has slipped this mortal coil.
You would think, after centuries of it, one would grow weary of the taste.
But that's the real reason we cultivate them, isn't it? Because *man* is so very *toothsome.*
Saved you some.

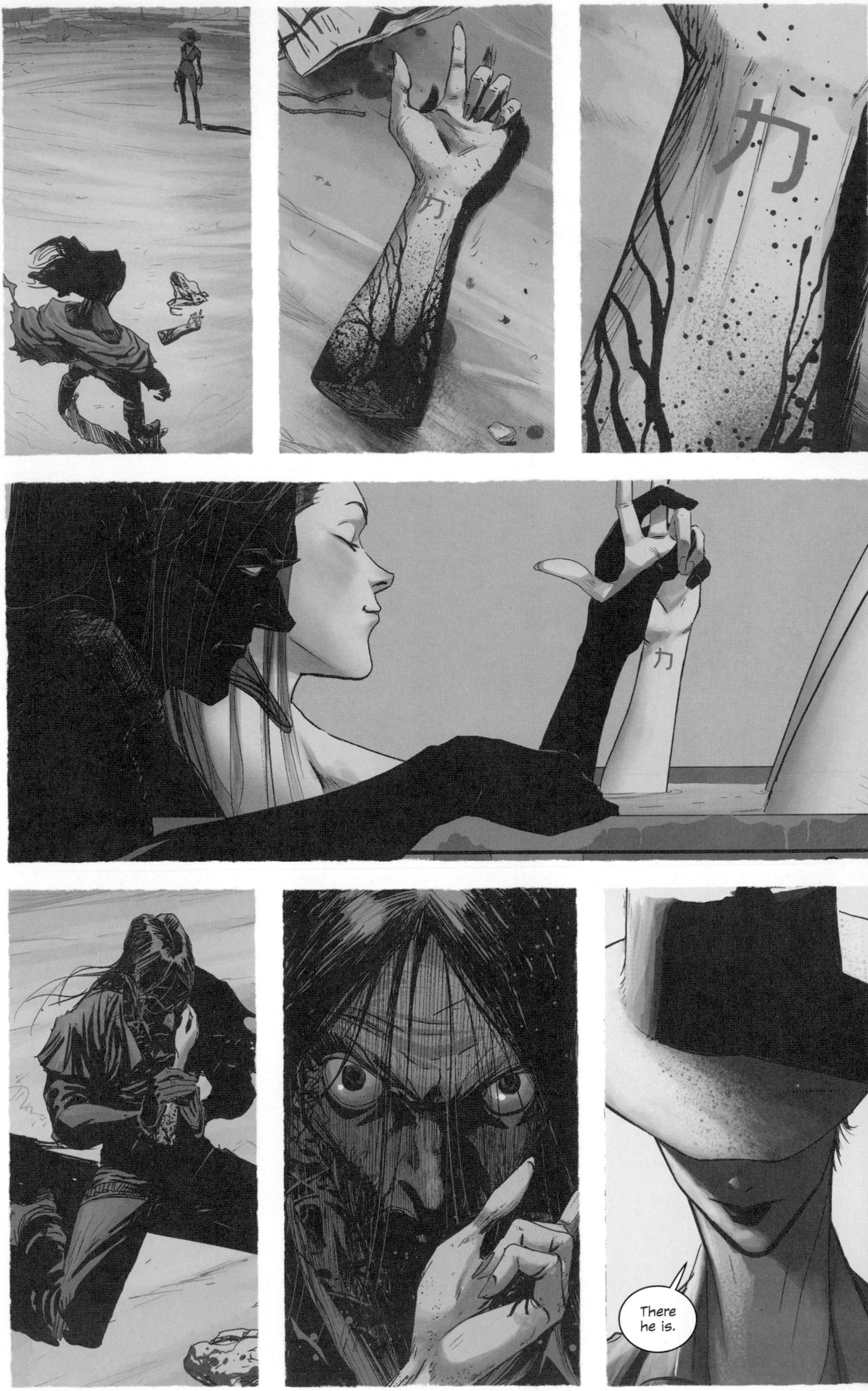
There he is.

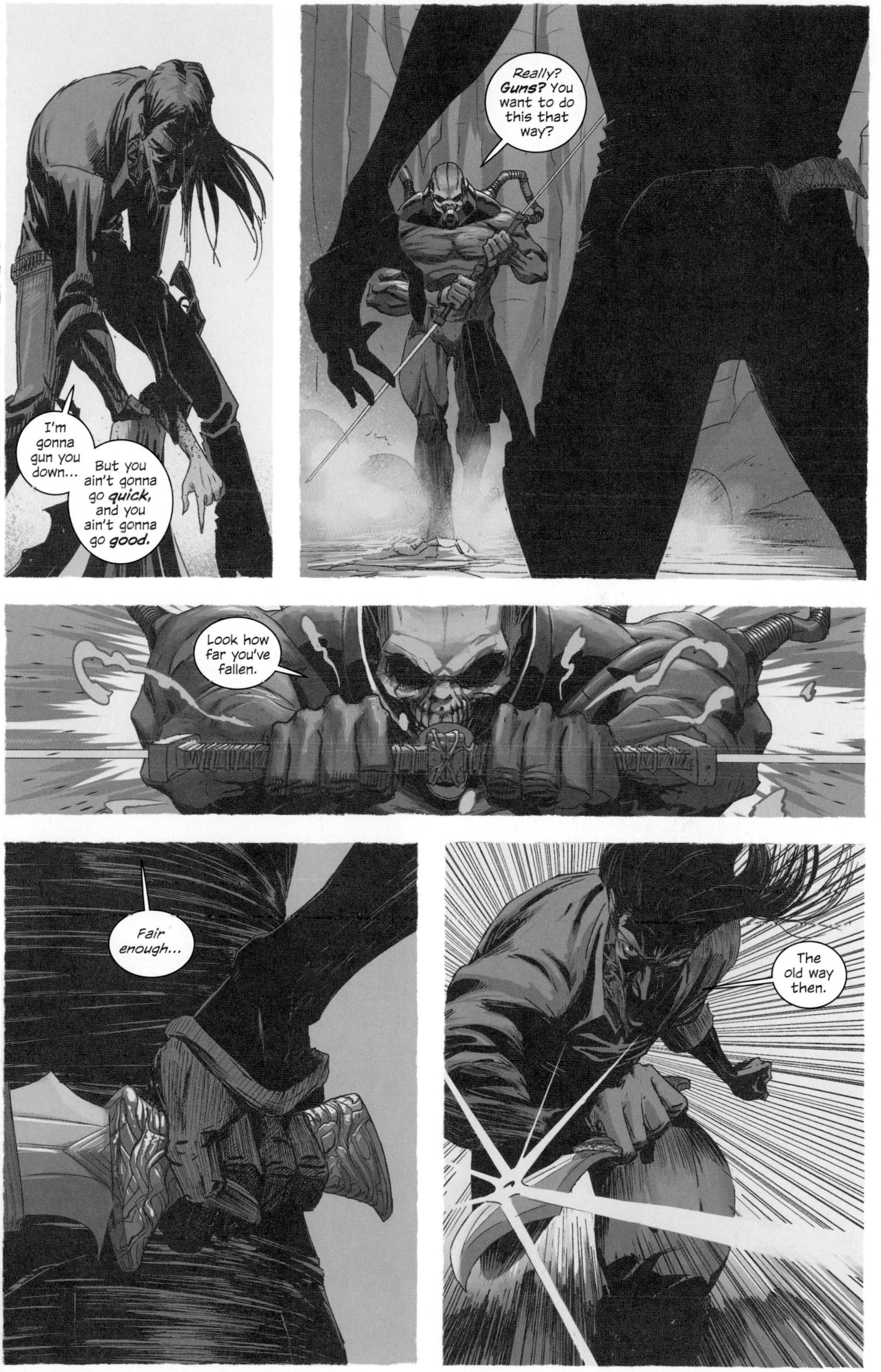
I'm gonna gun you down...
But you ain't gonna go *quick,* and you ain't gonna go *good.*
Really? ***Guns?*** You want to do this that way?
Look how far you've fallen.
Fair enough...
The old way then.

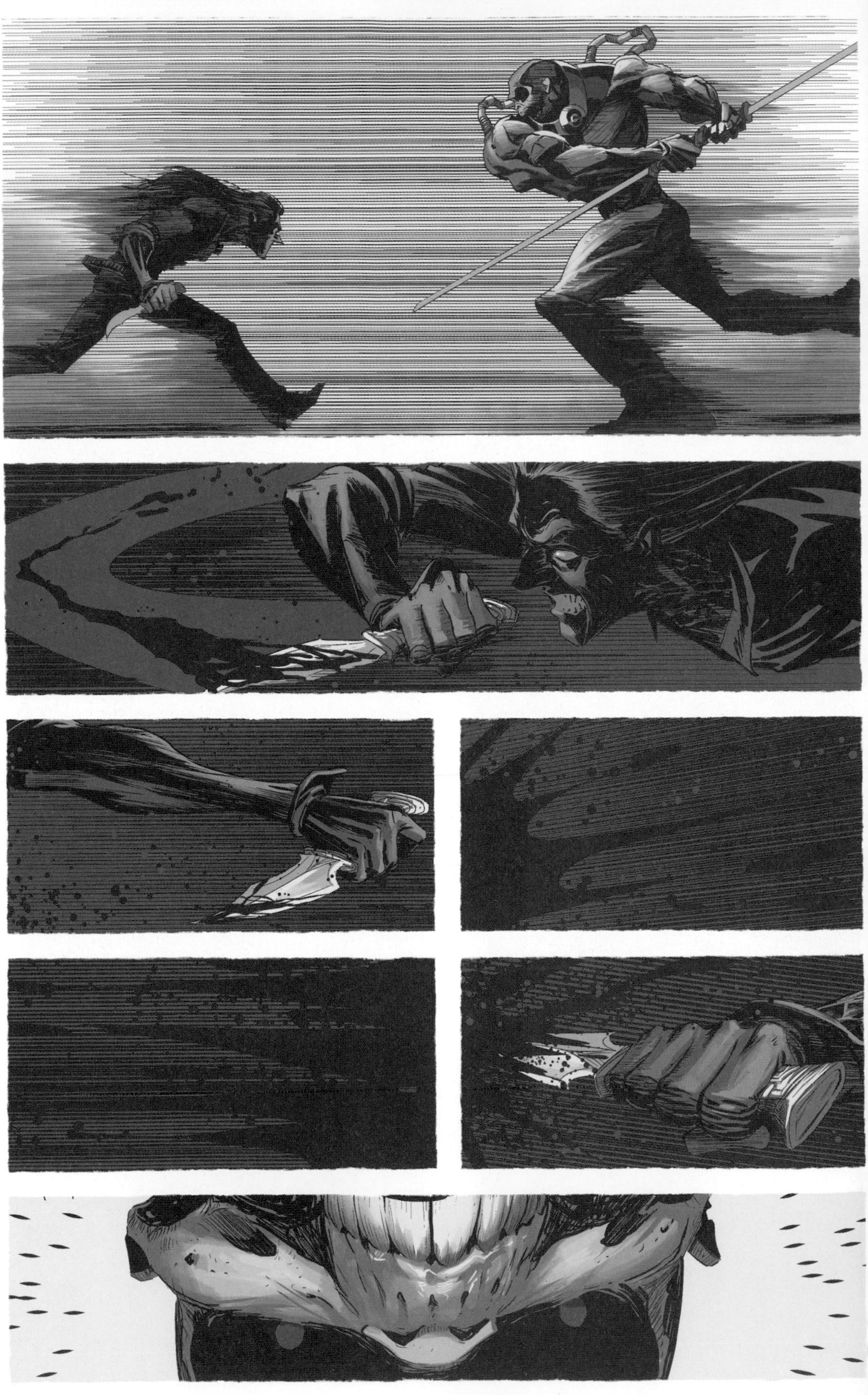

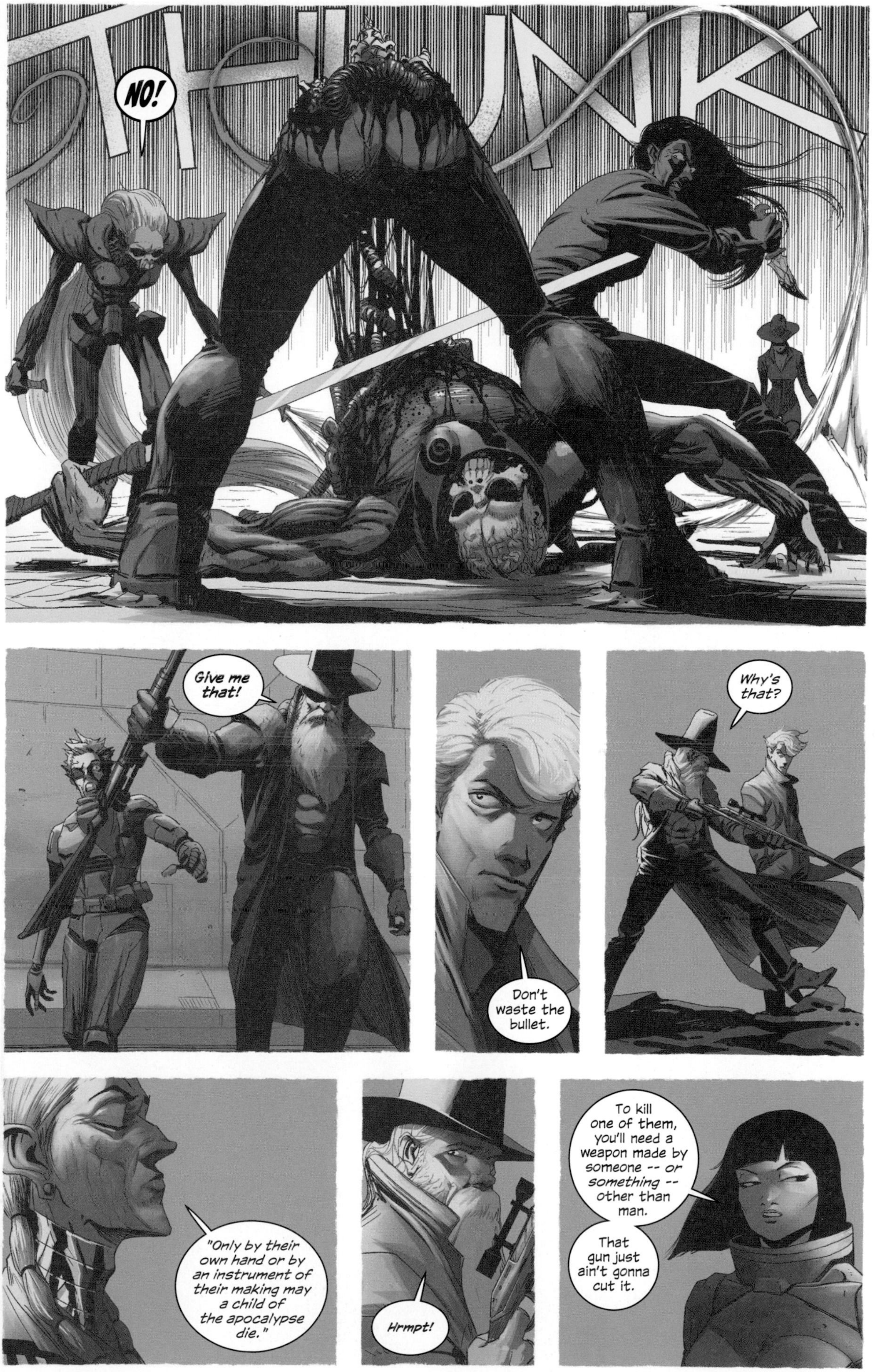
THUNK
NO!
Give me that!
Don't waste the bullet.
Why's that?
"Only by their own hand or by an instrument of their making may a child of the apocalypse die."
Hrmpt!
To kill one of them, you'll need a weapon made by someone -- or something -- other than man.
That gun just ain't gonna cut it.

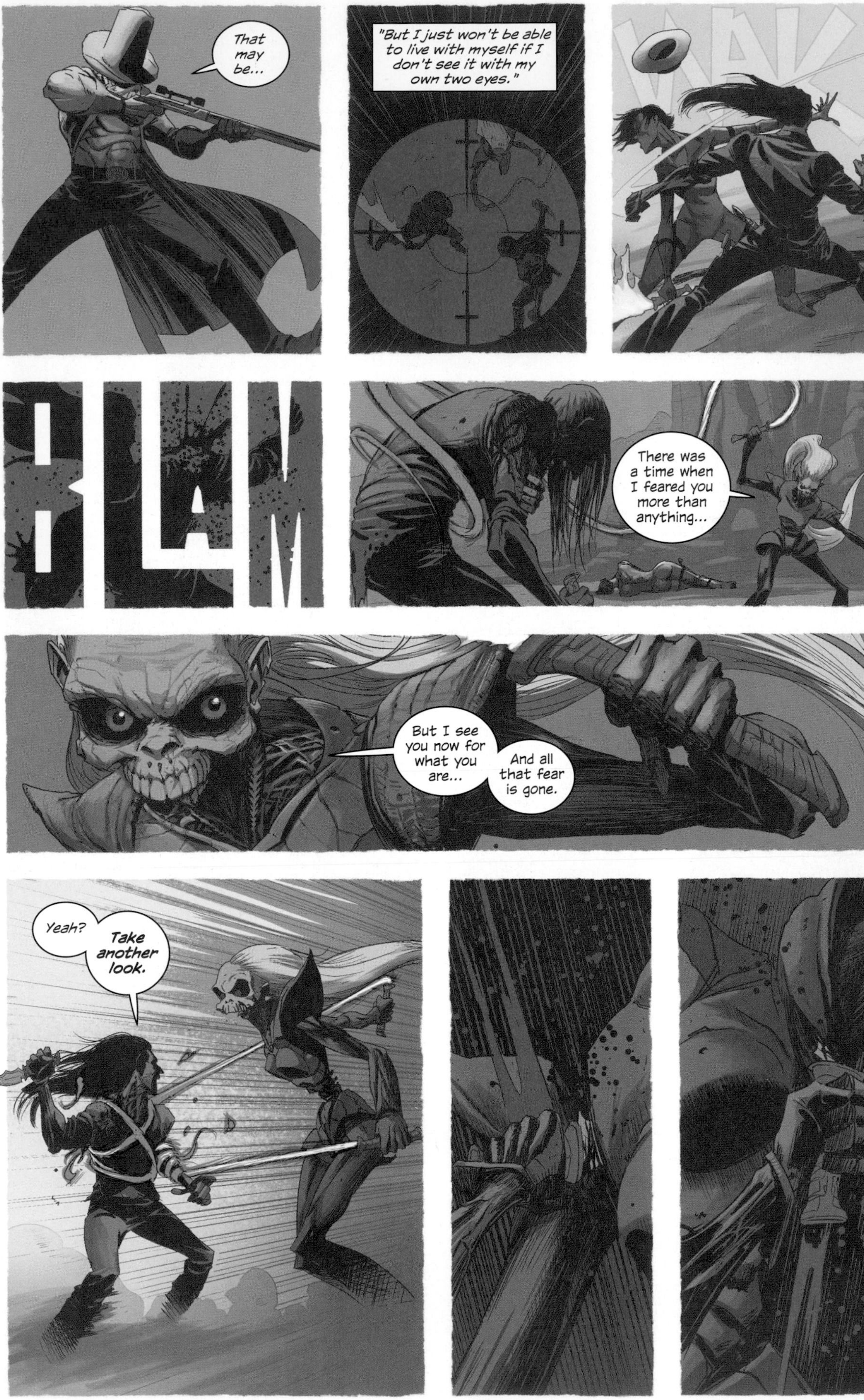
That may be...
"But I just won't be able to live with myself if I don't see it with my own two eyes."
BLAM
There was a time when I feared you more than anything...
But I see you now for what you are...
And all that fear is gone.
Yeah?
Take another look.

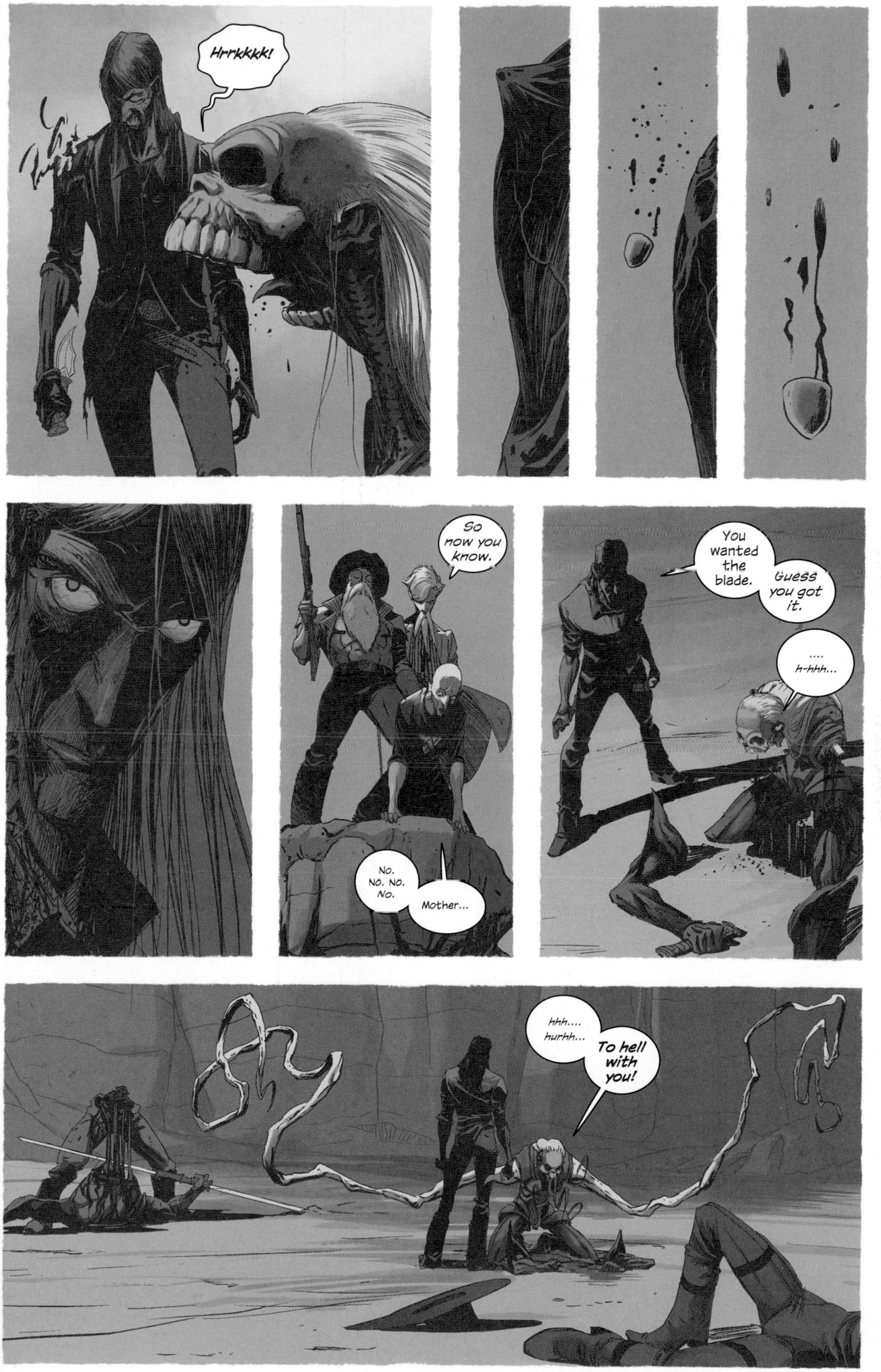
Hrrkkkk!
So now you know.
No. No. No. No.
Mother...
You wanted the blade.
Guess you got it.
.... h-hhh...
hhh.... hurhh...
To hell with you!

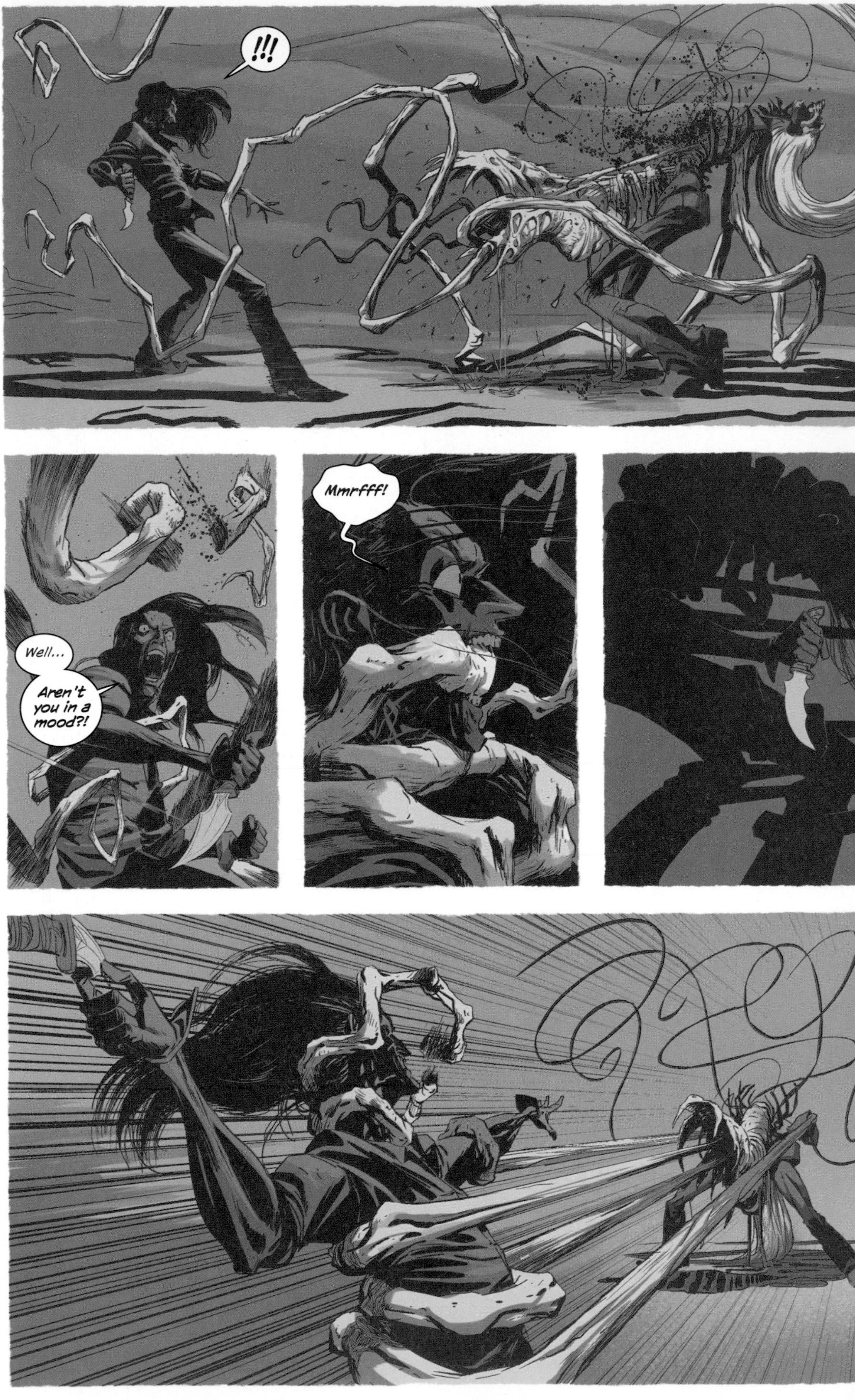
!!!
Well...
Aren't you in a mood?!
Mmrfff!

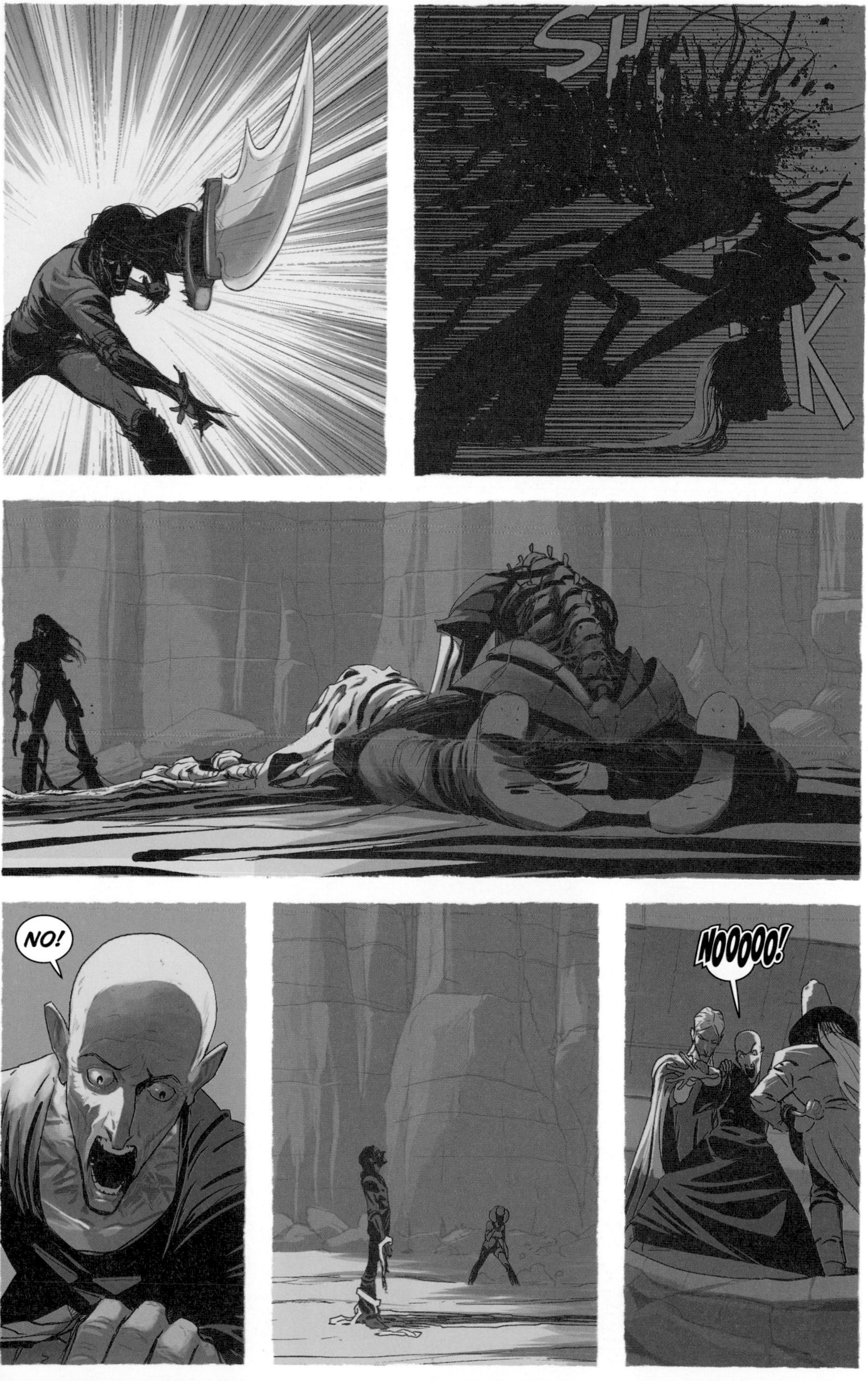
SHK
NO!
NOOOOO!

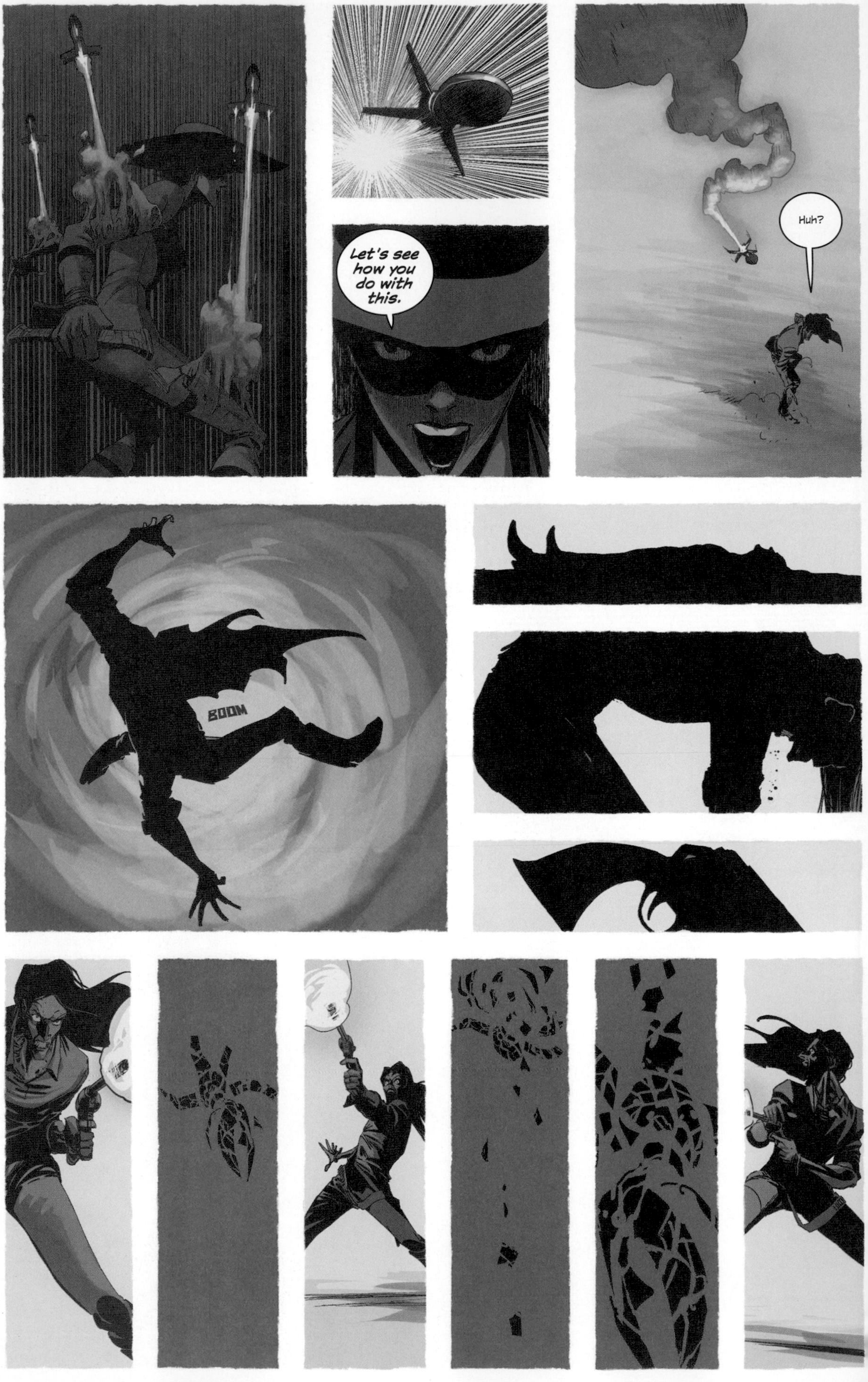
Let's see how you do with this.
Huh?
BOOM

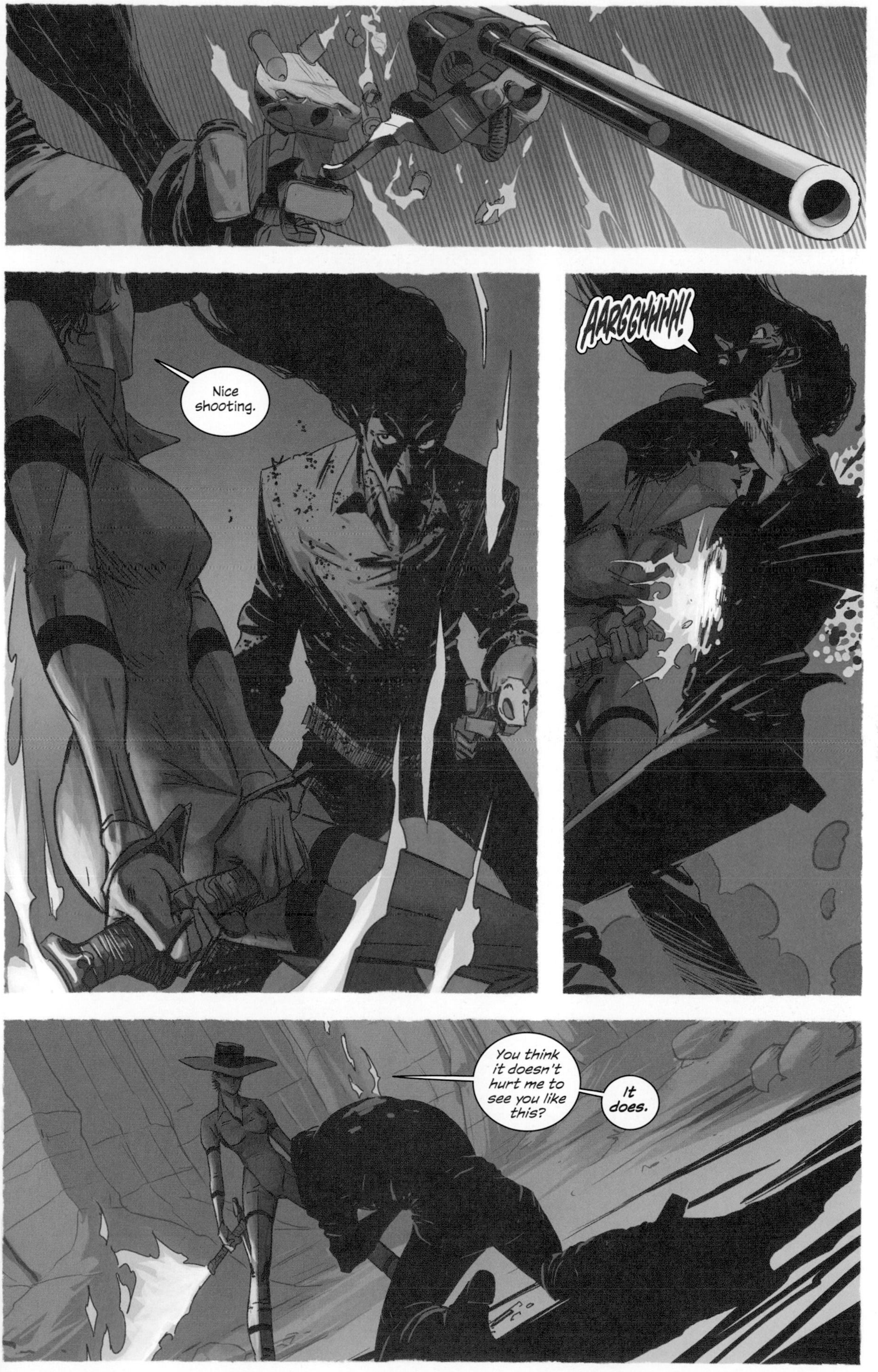

Nice shooting.
AARGGHHHH!
You think it doesn't hurt me to see you like this?
It does.

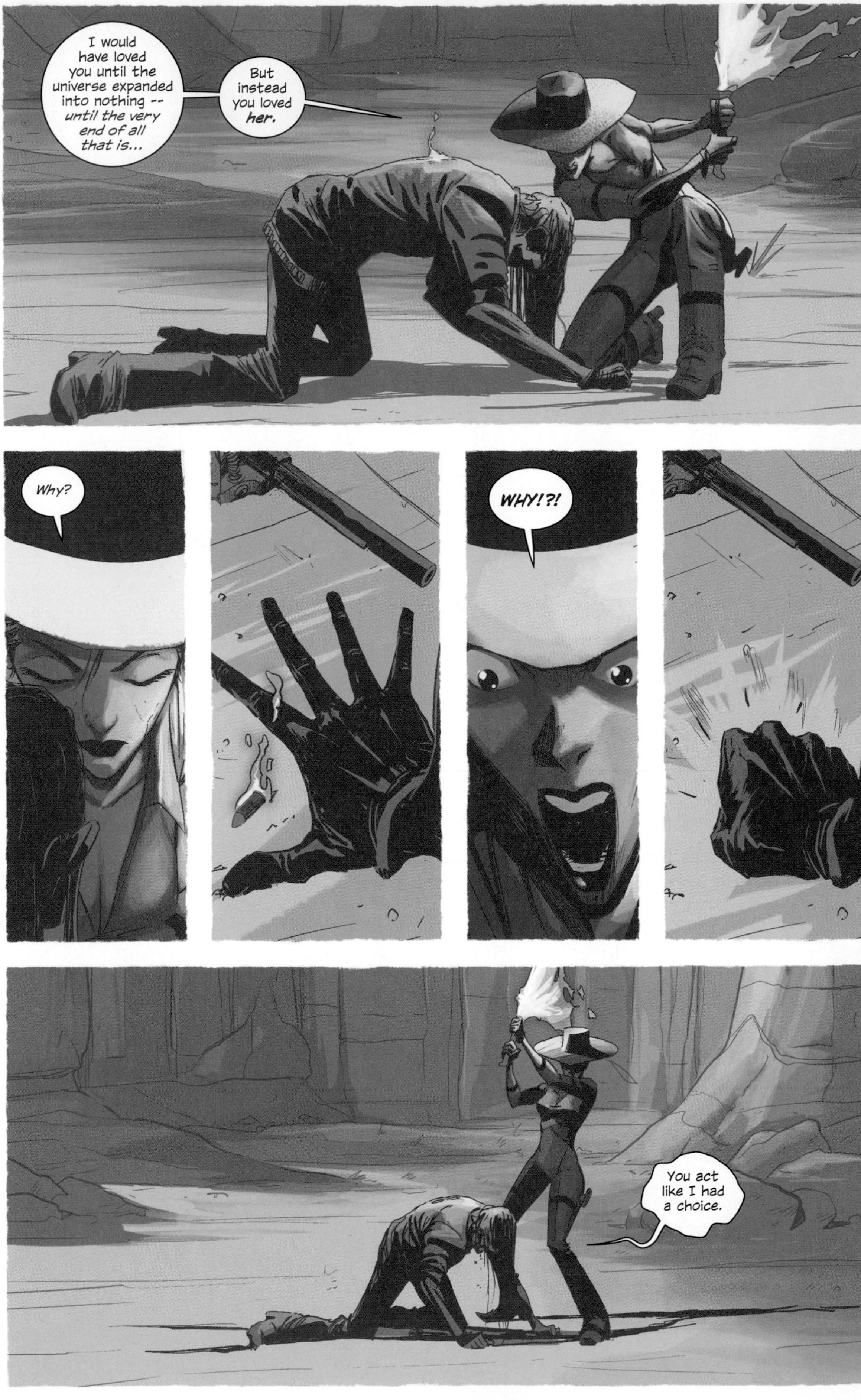
I would have loved you until the universe expanded into nothing -- until the very end of all that is...
But instead you loved her.
Why?
WHY!?!
You act like I had a choice.

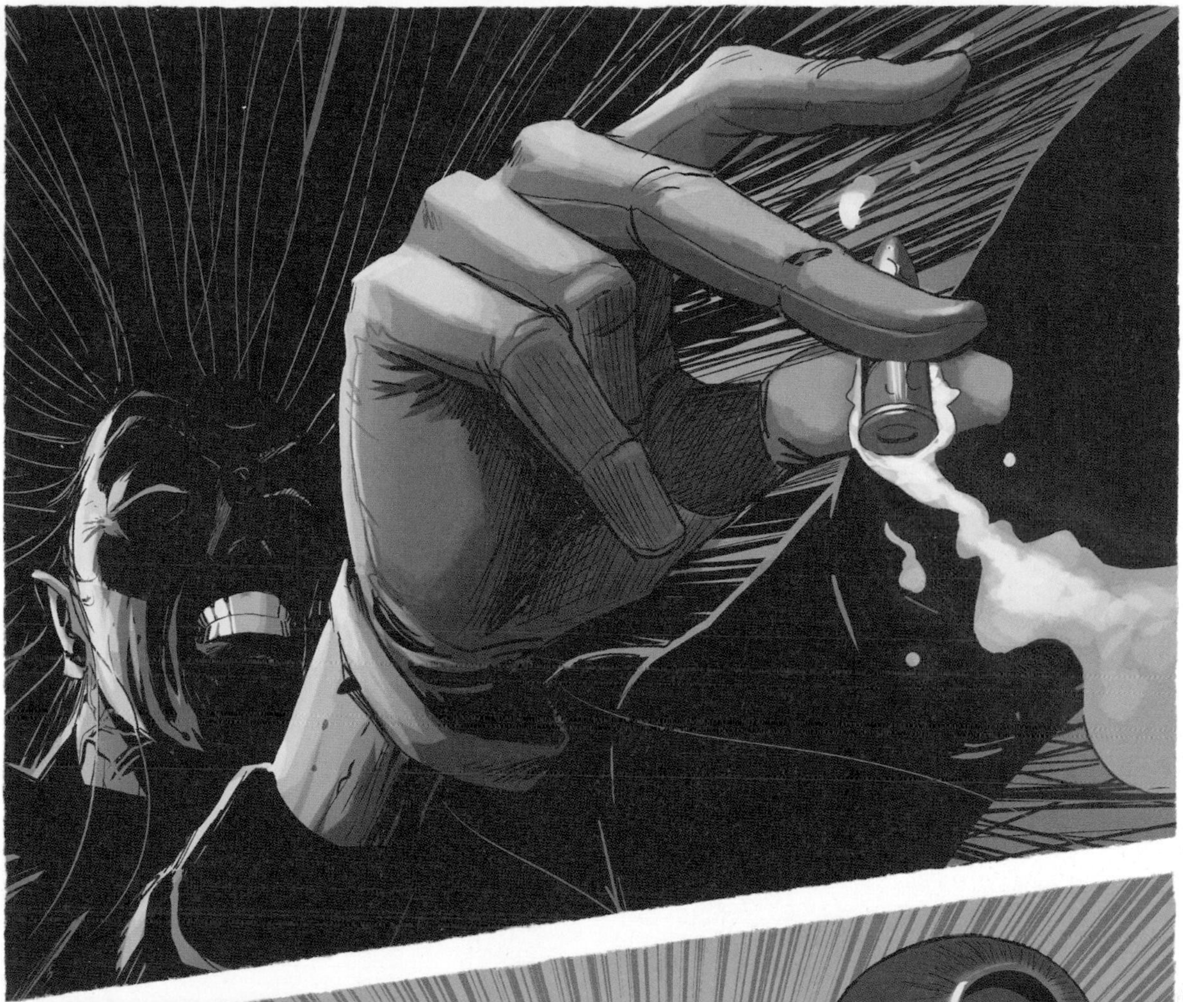

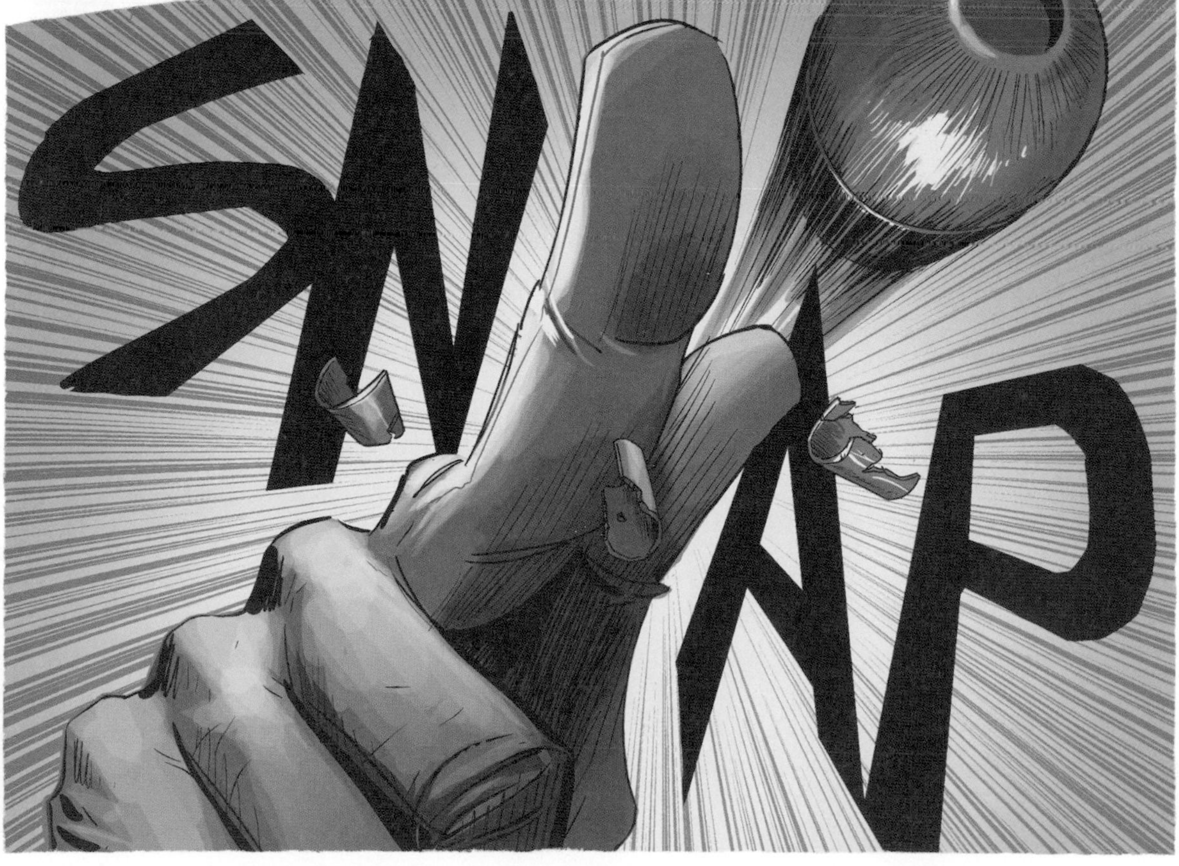
SNAP

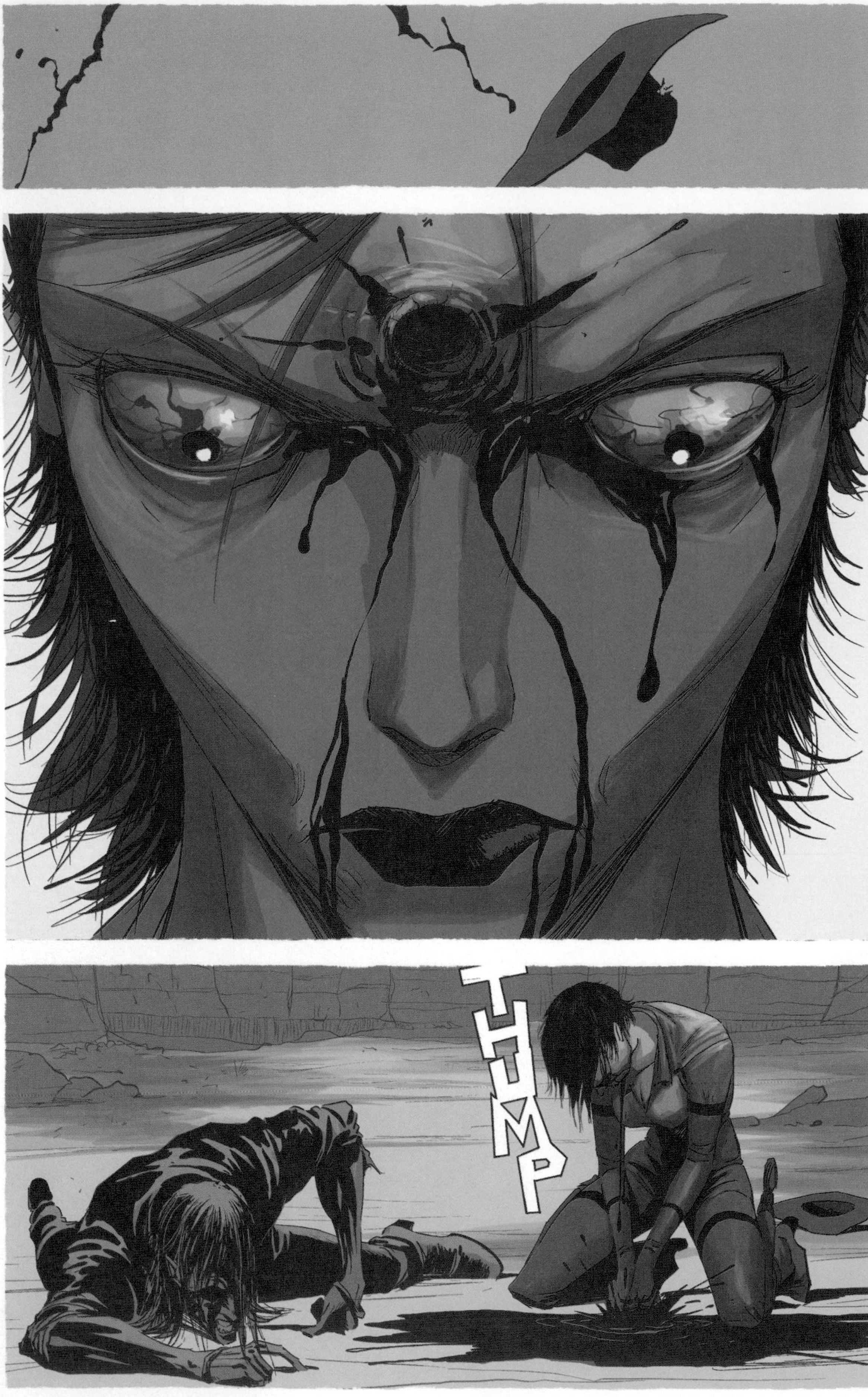
THUMP

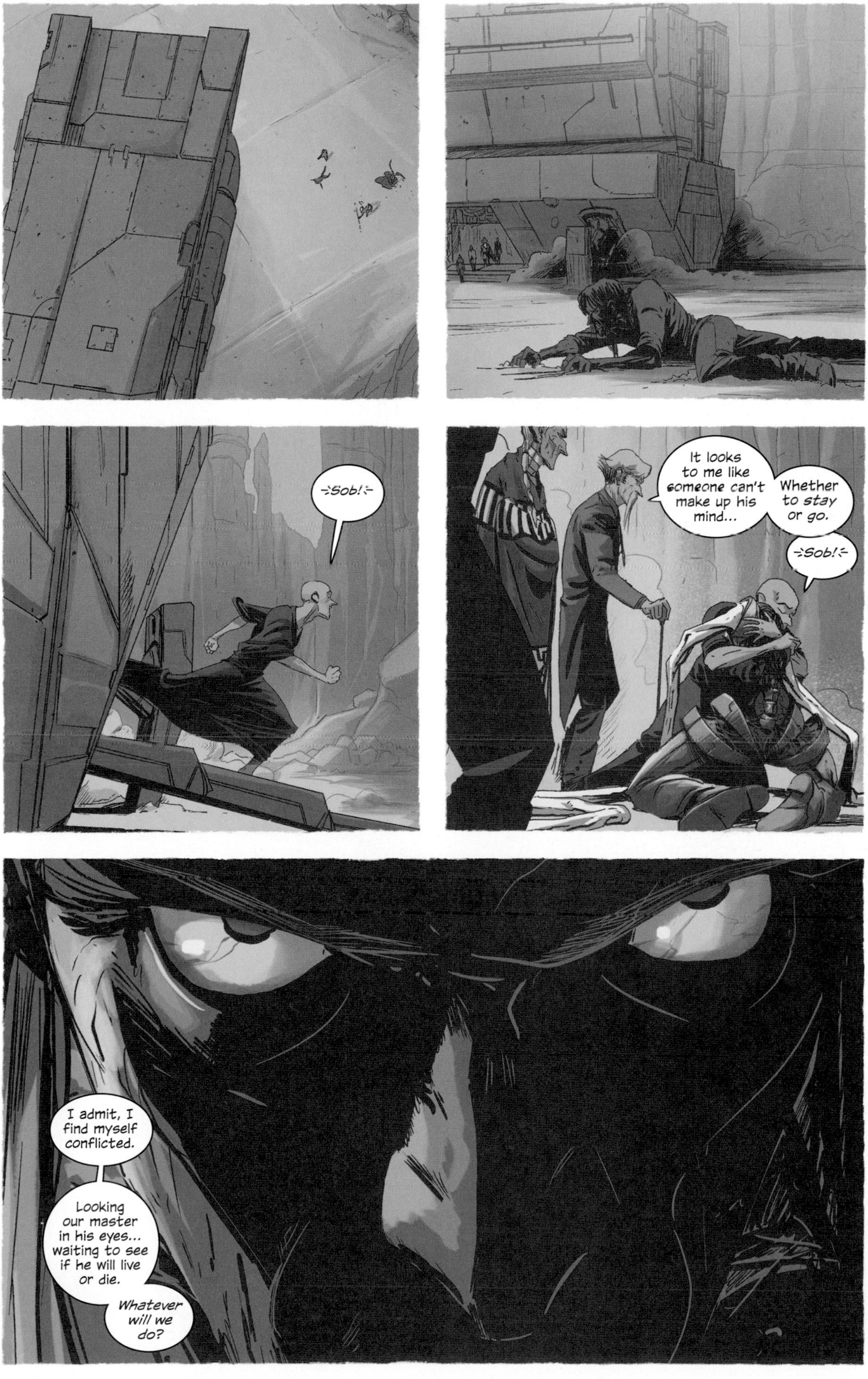
-Sob!-
It looks to me like someone can't make up his mind...
Whether to *stay* or go.
-Sob!-
I admit, I find myself conflicted.
Looking our master in his eyes... waiting to see if he will live or die.
Whatever will we do?

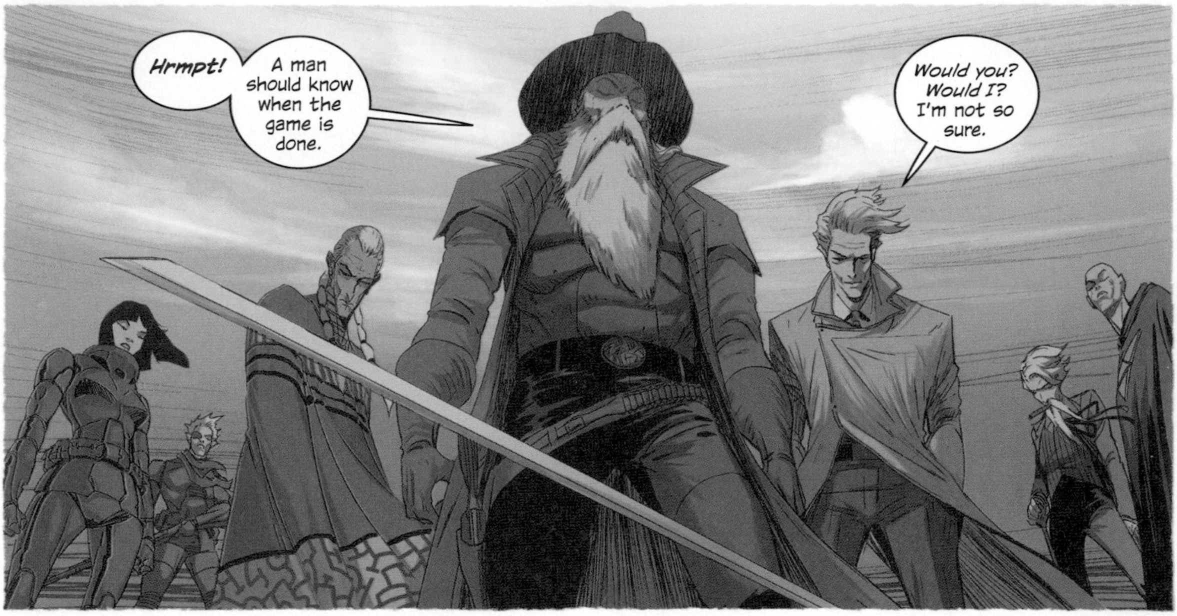
Hrmpt!
A man should know when the game is done.
Would you? Would I? I'm not so sure.

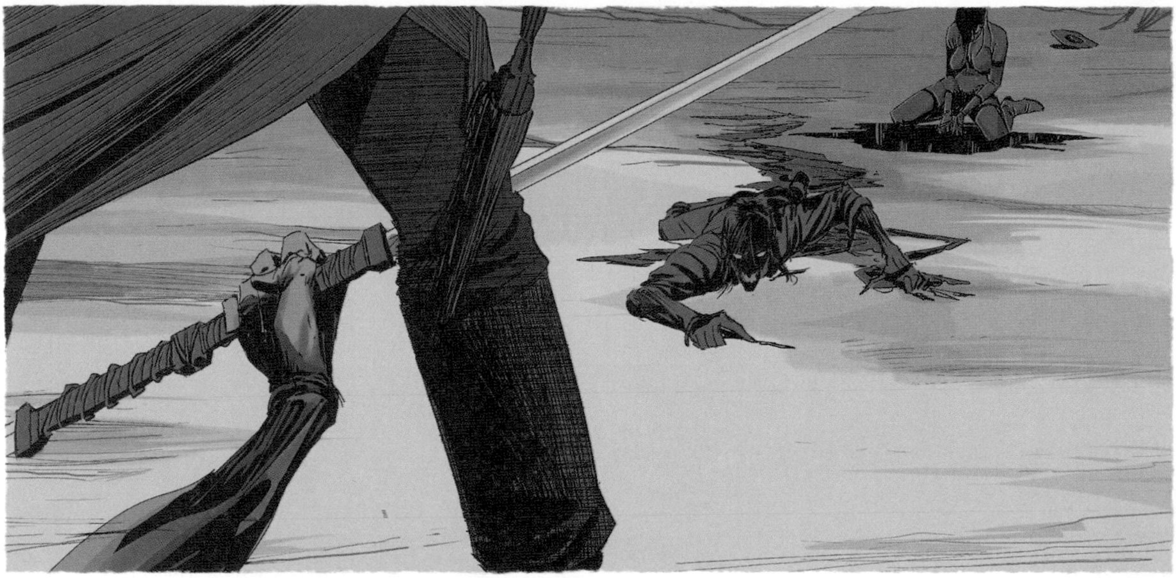

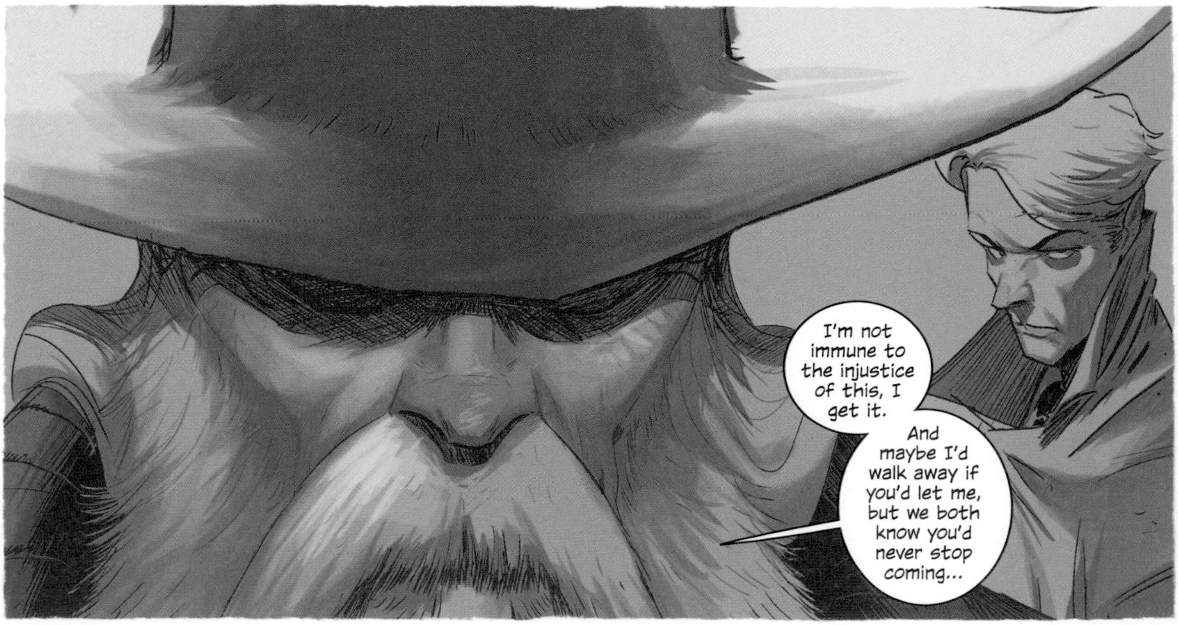
I'm not immune to the injustice of this, I get it.
And maybe I'd walk away if you'd let me, but we both know you'd never stop coming...

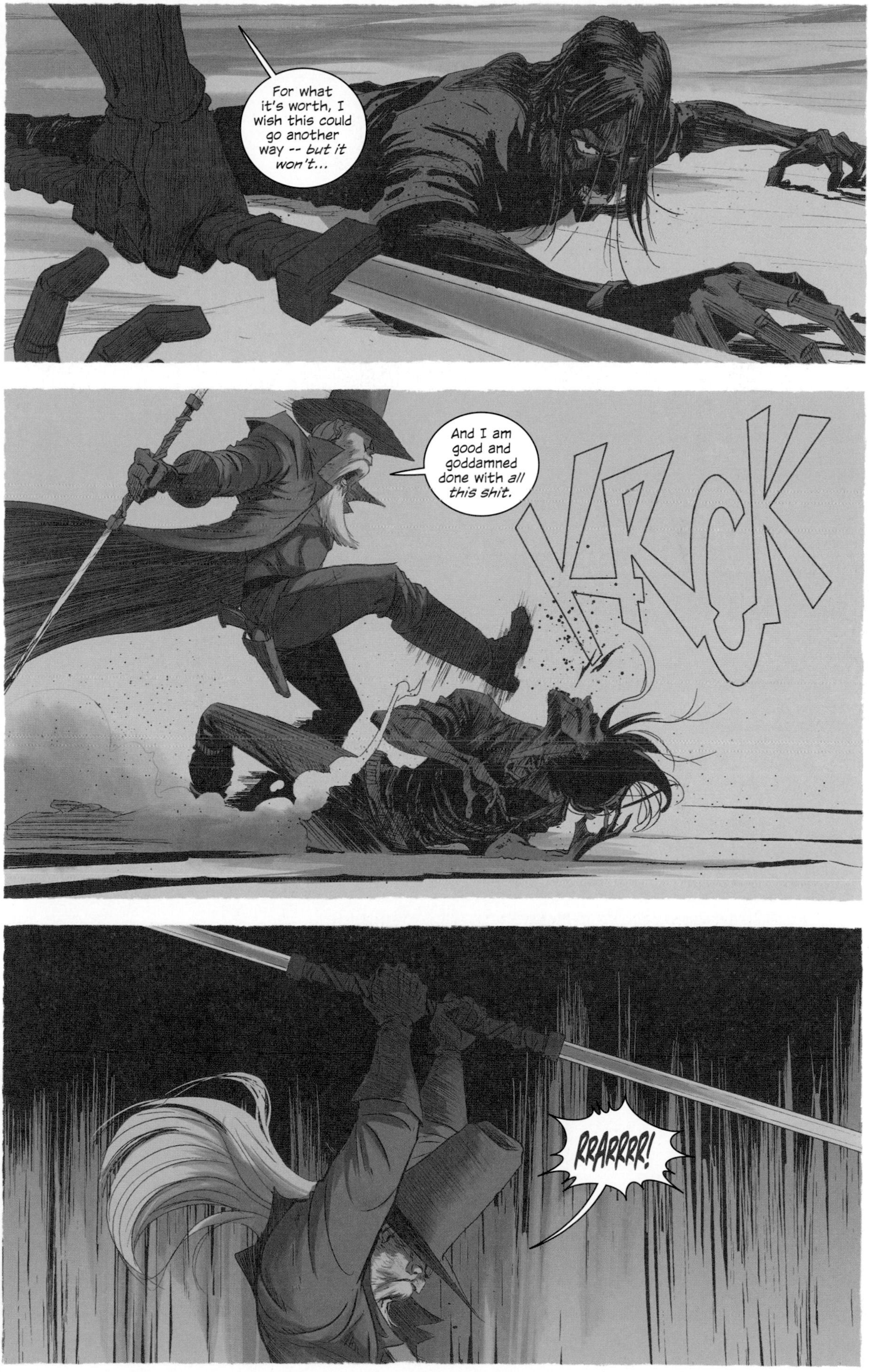
For what it's worth, I wish this could go another way -- *but it won't...*
And I am good and goddamned done with *all this shit.*
KRCK
RRARRRR!

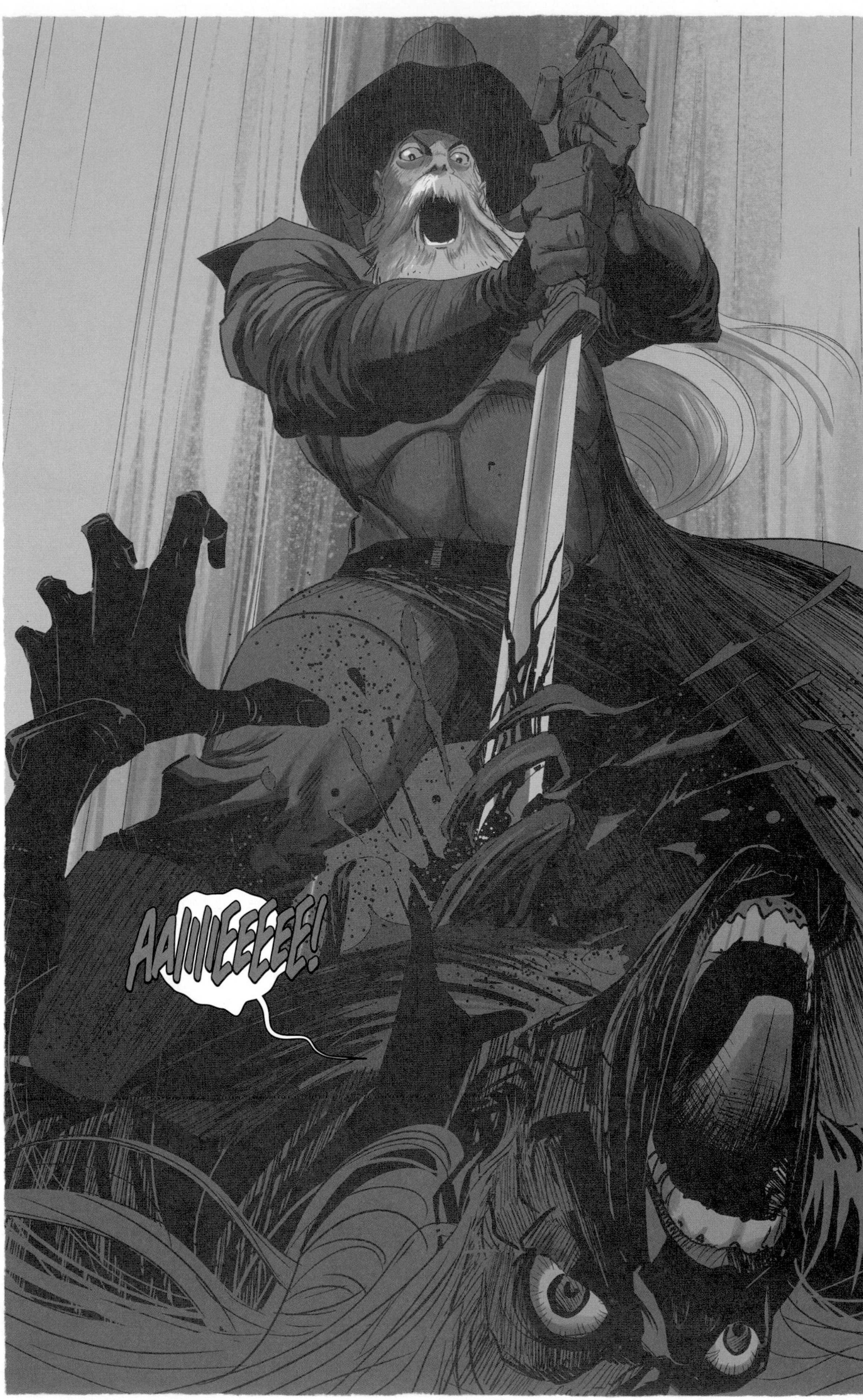
AAIIIIEEEEE!

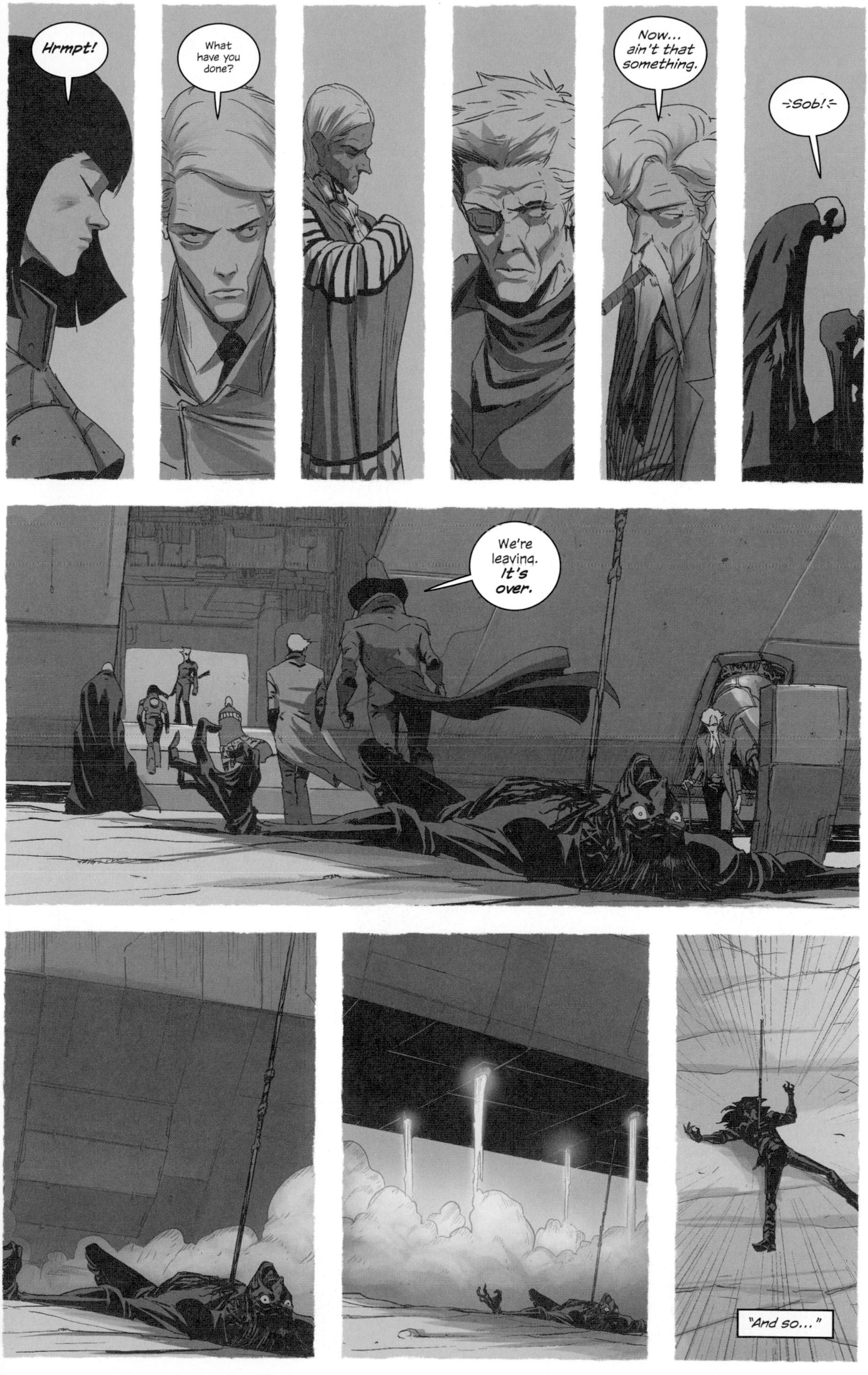
Hrmpt!
What have you done?
Now... ain't that something.
-Sob!-
We're leaving. It's over.
"And so..."

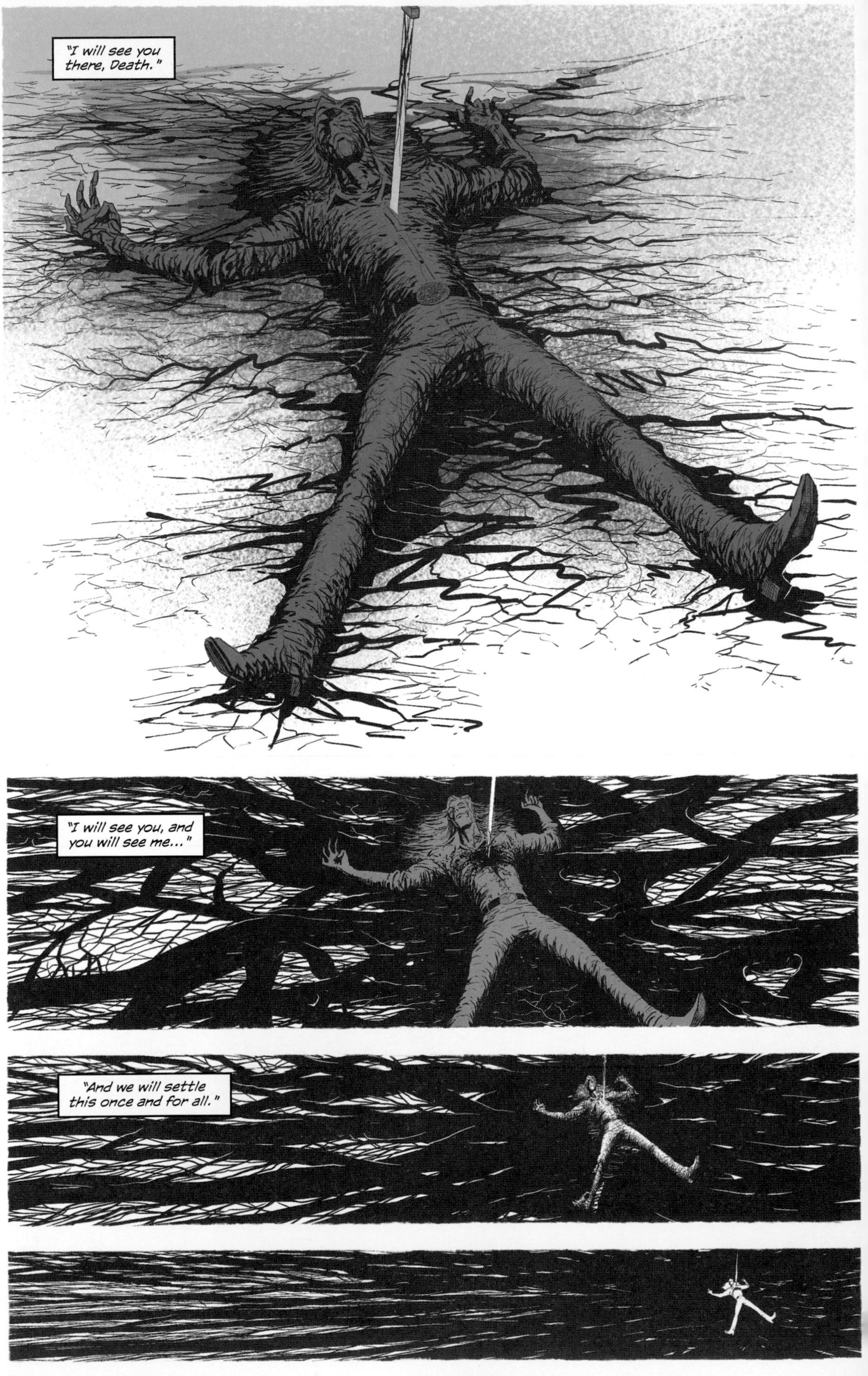
"I will see you there, Death."
"I will see you, and you will see me..."
"And we will settle this once and for all."

ALL MEN TELL **LIES.**
THESE ARE A **FEW** OF
THEM.

Jonathan Hickman is the visionary talent behind such works as the Eisner-nominated **NIGHTLY NEWS**, **THE MANHATTAN PROJECTS** and **PAX ROMANA**. He also plies his trade at MARVEL working on books like **FANTASTIC FOUR** and **THE AVENGERS**.

His twin brother, Marc, was one of the founders of bitcoin but only pays for things in cash.

Jonathan lives in South Carolina most of the time.

You can visit his website: **www.pronea.com**, or email him at: **jonathan@pronea.com**.

·

Nick Dragotta's career began at Marvel Comics working on titles as varied as **X-STATIX, THE AGE OF THE SENTRY, X-MEN: FIRST CLASS, CAPTAIN AMERICA: FOREVER ALLIES** and **VENGEANCE**.

In addition, Nick is the co-creator of **HOWTOONS,** a comic series teaching kids how to build things and explore the world around them. **EAST OF WEST** is Nick's first creator-owned project at Image.